HEAVENLY
FEASTS

HEAVENLY FEASTS

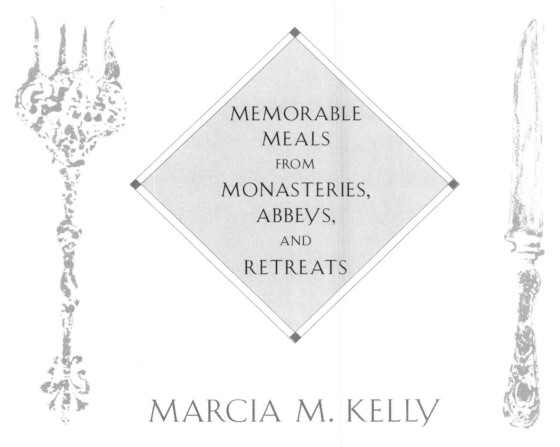

MEMORABLE
MEALS
FROM
MONASTERIES,
ABBEYS,
AND
RETREATS

MARCIA M. KELLY

ILLUSTRATIONS BY EDITH FEUERSTEIN SCHROT

BELL TOWER ☖ NEW YORK

Published by Bell Tower, an imprint of Harmony Books, a division of Crown Publishers, Inc., 201 East 50th Street, New York, New York 10022. Member of the Crown Publishing Group.

Random House, Inc. New York, Toronto, London, Sydney, Auckland

http://www.randomhouse.com/

Harmony, Bell Tower, and colophon are trademarks of Crown Publishers, Inc.

Printed in the United States of America

Design by Nancy Kenmore

Library of Congress Cataloging-in-Publication Data
is available upon request.

ISBN 0-517-88522-0

10 9 8 7 6 5 4 3 2 1

First Edition

A percentage of the royalties from this book will go to Project Reachout, the program of Goddard-Riverside Community Center in New York City that works with homeless people who are mentally ill.

CONTENTS

◆

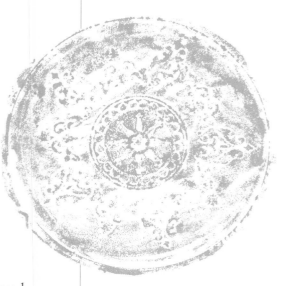

Saint Mary's Episcopal Retreat
and Conference Center
Sewanee, Tennessee

A FAVORITE BREAKFAST 15

Cheese Grits

Sour Cream–Cinnamon Breakfast Cake

fruit and yogurt

Springwater Center
Springwater, New York

WINTER BREAKFAST 17

Hot Oatmeal

Homemade Yogurt · Stewed Prunes and Apricots

warm orange-blossom honey · fresh fruit

Apple-Mint Tea

BRUNCHES, LUNCHES, AND DINNERS 19

Abbey of New Clairvaux
Vina, California

A FARM MONASTERY VEGETARIAN FEAST 21

Corn Casserole · Oven-Browned Potatoes · Risotto

Brother Gerard's Biscuit Twisters · Sweet-and-Sour Carrot

Salad · tossed green salad with pea pods, broccoli florets,

baby carrots, and cauliflower · Prune Cake

Avila Retreat Center
Durham, North Carolina

VALENTINE-EVENING DINNER 26
fresh strawberry fruit cup · Estella's Squash Casserole
peas and mushrooms · small green salad · Cheese Biscuits
Bread Pudding with Hard Sauce

Bhavana Society
High View, West Virginia

SOUP AND SALAD 29
Lima Bean Soup · Homemade Wheat Bread
tossed salad with Hollyhock Dressing

Breitenbush Hot Springs
Detroit, Oregon

A SOUTHWESTERN MEAL 32
Yam-and-Jalapeño Enchiladas · Tomatillo Sauce
fresh salsa · organic blue corn chips

Camp Weed and Cerveny
Conference Center
Live Oak, Florida

A PLANTATION PARTY 34
Low-Country Boil · lots of beer and lemonade

Dai Bosatsu Zendo
Livingston Manor, New York

THREE-BOWL MEAL *JIHATSU* 35
Ginger Rice · Hot-and-Sour Baked Tofu
Seiko's Noodles with Spinach, Carrots, and Eggs

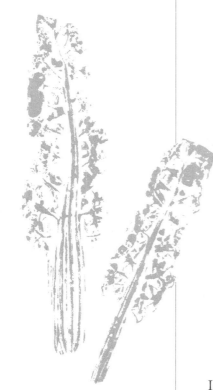

Falkynor Farm
Davie, Florida

A TROPICAL SUPPER 38

Lime Stew · Green Papaya Coleslaw

Mango Ice Cream

PIZZA PARTY 42

Tomato-Veggie Pizza · Miso-Veggie Pizza

Potato-Fennel Pizza · Fresh Fruit "Gello"

Abbey of Gethsemani
Trappist, Kentucky

A MONK'S MEAL 47

Corn Chowder · Cabbage and Polenta

Brother Ambrose's Biscuits

The Healing Center of Arizona
Sedona, Arizona

SUNDAY SUPPER IN ARIZONA 51

Enchilada Casserole · Herbed Mushroom Rice

Ignacia's Bean Salad · Isleta's Rice Pudding with Apricots

Holy Name Monastery
St. Leo, Florida

TRADITIONAL NEW YEAR'S DINNER 55

Baked Ham with Orange Glaze · Black-eyed Peas

Sweet Potatoes · Collard Greens

Cucumber-and-Tomato Salad with Cream Dressing

Corn Bread · Southern Pecan Pie

Immaculate Heart Community
Santa Barbara, California
COMMUNITY SUPPER 61
Celebration Spaghetti · Chinese Coleslaw

Chocolate Chip Cookies

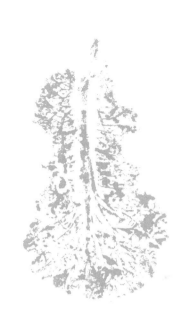

Insight Meditation Society
Barre, Massachusetts
SILENT RETREAT SUPPER 64
Mushroom-Almond-Rice Casserole · Baked Carrots and

Parsnips · Steamed Kale · Green Salad

Beyond Greens Dressing · Pears with Raisin Sauce

Mepkin Abbey
Moncks Corner, South Carolina
A MONK'S FEAST 68
Frittata with salsa · Garden Corn Salad

Green Salad with Father Aelred's Mother's Dressing

Sun-dried Tomato Pesto with Pasta · Corn Bread Casserole

Brother Boniface's French Bread

Pendle Hill
Wallingford, Pennsylvania
A QUAKER EARLY AUTUMN MENU 73
Carol Ryan's Baked Italian Vegetable Casserole with Polenta

Pendle Hill Bread

Green Salad with Balsamic Garlic Vinaigrette

A QUAKER SUMMER MENU 77

Tina Tau's Chicken with Orange and Walnuts

Baked Yams · Steamed Fresh Green Beans

Pendle Hill Cheese Pie

Portsmouth Abbey
Portsmouth, Rhode Island

FAVORITE RECIPES 80

Clam Chowder · Mushrooms à la Grecque

Roast Duckling à l'Orange · Roast Leg of Lamb

Hermits

Rancho La Puerta
Tecate, Baja California, Mexico

A FESTIVE DINNER 86

Mexican Roasted Corn Soup

Jícama, Red Onion, and Orange Salad

Chilies Rellenos with Salsa Ranchera Colorado,

Mexican Rice, and Black Bean Frijoles

Strawberry-Banana Sorbet

Rose Hill
Aiken, South Carolina

FOURTH OF JULY SOUTH CAROLINA BARBECUE 94

Slow-Roasted Pig · Mustard Barbecue Sauce

South Carolina Hash · white rice · sliced white bread

coleslaw · Chocolate Pear Tart

Saint Christopher Conference Center
Charleston, South Carolina

ANNUAL CLERGY CONFERENCE
BRUNCH 98

Low-Country She-Crab Soup with Sherry · Crab, Spinach,
Swiss, and Onion Quiche · Charleston Shrimp and Grits
with Bacon Strips and Sliced Tomatoes · Buttermilk
Biscuits · Saint Christopher Mud Pie · Huguenot Torte

Saint Francis Friends of the Poor
New York, New York

AN ITALIAN BUFFET 104

Escarole Soup with Meatballs · *Penne al Pomodoro e Basilico*
Bruschetta · Chicken and Potatoes · Spinach and Beans
fresh fruit and cheese

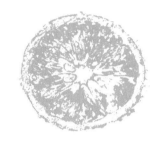

Saint Mary's Episcopal Retreat and
Conference Center
Sewanee, Tennessee

BOARD LUNCHEON 109

Cream Cheese Lasagna · Homemade Rolls · tossed salad
with Poppy Seed Dressing · Quick Peanut-Butter Fudge

Southern Dharma Retreat Center
Hot Springs, North Carolina

SIMPLY HEALTHFUL 113

Oh You Beautiful Dal · Spelt Bread · green salad with
Tahini-Basil Dressing · Favorite Brownies

Transfiguration Monastery
Windsor, New York

HOLIDAY FEAST 117
Basque Shrimp and Mushrooms in White Wine
Roast Chicken · Vegetables from Bordeaux-Basque Cuisine
Strawberry Compote

SUNDAY SUPPER 122
Vegetable Soup · Banana or Raisin Omelette
Salade Niçoise

Villa Maria Del Mar
Santa Cruz, California

SUNSET FEAST BY THE SEA 124
Lemon Chicken with Thyme · Vegetable Polenta · Napa
Cabbage Salad · Cheesecake with Fresh Raspberries

Visitation Monastery
Mobile, Alabama

SUNDAY DINNER 129
Oven-Baked Southern Chicken · rice and Gravy
peas · Tomato Aspic and dressing · rolls and butter
Apple Crisp

Wakulla Springs Lodge
Wakulla Springs, Florida

WAKULLA SPRINGS LODGE BUFFET 133
Navy Bean Soup · Crab Imperial · Wakulla Shrimp
Supreme · Whole Baked Tomatoes with hush puppies
Fluffy Lime Cream Pie · Blueberry—Sour Cream Pie

RECImport: RECIPES BY CATEGORY

◆

BREAKFAST
Apple-Mint Tea, 18
Applenola, 4
Breakfast Casserole, 3
Buttermilk Pancakes, 158
Cheese Grits, 15
Genmai, 12
Gomasio, 14
Granola, 156
Kukuye Sabzi, 11
Melt-in-the-Mouth Cookies, 6
Müsli, 7
Oatmeal, 17
Overnight Baked Porridge, 8
Stewed Prunes and Apricots,
    18
Yogurt (The Hermitage), 9
Yogurt (Springwater Center),
    18

BREADS
Brother Ambrose's Biscuits, 50
Brother Boniface's French
    Bread, 72
Brother Gerard's Biscuit
    Twisters, 23
Bruschetta, 107
Buttermilk Biscuits, 102
Cheese Biscuits, 27
Corn Bread, 59
Delicious Bran Muffins, 157
Homemade Rolls, 110
Homemade Wheat Bread, 30

Oatmeal Bread, 5
Pendle Hill Bread, 75
Pumpkin Bread, 5
Sour Cream–Cinnamon
    Breakfast Cake, 16
Spelt Bread, 115

SALADS AND DRESSINGS
Balsamic Garlic Vinaigrette, 76
Barley-Corn Salad, 140
Beyond Greens Dressing, 67
Chinese Coleslaw, 62
Cucumber-and-Tomato Salad
    with Cream Dressing, 58
Darrel's Favorite Dressing, 161
Father Aelred's Mother's
    Dressing, 70
Garden Corn Salad, 69
Green Papaya Coleslaw, 40
Hollyhock Dressing, 31
Ignacia's Bean Salad, 53
Jícama, Red Onion, and
    Orange Salad, 87
Napa Cabbage Salad, 127
Poppy Seed Dressing, 111
Salade Niçoise, 123
Tahini-Basil Dressing, 115
Tomato Aspic, 131

SOUPS
Clam Chowder, 80
Corn Chowder, 48

SPECIAL THANKS

◆

To my sister, Connie Brothers, for her wise, cheerful, and never-ending help, this time sending me Curt Mark, who tested and tasted these recipes with discernment; to Toinette Lippe, an amazing and wonderful editor; to Mary Cygan, for tireless word processing, even with a newborn baby at her side; to all those who kindly took the time and energy to write out their delicious menus and recipes for this book; and to Jack, my favorite traveling companion.

INTRODUCTION

•

As many of you know, in the late 1980s my husband, Jack, and I began a journey that has led us, so far, to more than 250 monasteries, abbeys, and retreats in this country. Tangible results of these travels have been our book series, *Sanctuaries: A Guide to Lodgings in Monasteries, Abbeys, and Retreats,* and our collection of mealtime blessings, *One Hundred Graces.* Unexpected tangible results were the extra pounds we seemed to gain after each trip. That had always happened as we searched out great restaurants on our travels over the years, but this was a spiritual journey, and what we hoped to acquire shouldn't have been so readily apparent!

Despite our interest in delicious food, what seemed to stand out at most monasteries were the people, the prayer life, the architecture, and the peaceful and beautiful surroundings. The food wasn't often what was most memorable. But in some places, the food seemed to embody the spirit of the place and made our spirits soar.

For this book I've returned to those special places and collected menus and recipes that are their own favorites. In the "Breakfasts" section you'll find everything from a holiday breakfast of Episcopal nuns, to a hearty Mennonite breakfast, to a vegetarian breakfast casserole from an Egyptian oasis in California. The "Brunches, Lunches, and Dinners" section includes feasts both large and small, austere and sumptuous. Following the monastic tradition of hospitality, where there's always a place at the table for anyone who appears at the door, many of these recipes will serve at least six to eight people. Assuming few readers will have occasion to entertain thirty monks, I've cut menus like "A Monastery Vegetarian Feast for Thirty Monks" down to manageable size. Though some of the menus are for special occasions, often the monasteries shared the recipes they most enjoy eating, whether guests are present or not.

Most cookbooks celebrate one cuisine—French, Indian, Italian, vegetarian, Southern—or one category—desserts, soups, pastas—but this book celebrates them all. When I told friends I was collecting recipes for a monastery cookbook, one of them laughed and said, "Oh, lots of dry bread and water, I'd expect!"

Contrary to her expectations, I discovered a wide variety of cooking styles and approaches. Just as each household reflects its own tastes, origins, and geography, so too do monasteries, abbeys, and retreats. We encountered world-class master chefs, French nuns carrying on family cooking traditions, simple and elaborate vegetarian menus, old-style Southern cooking, and even Southwestern fare. Our journeys took us to places of many different spiritual paths, and the food served turned out to be an amazing reflection of the nourishment we were offered at another level. In the end it's sustenance for us all which we are delighted to share with you.

Mealtime blessings are a tradition at many of the places we visited, and as we traveled we began to collect those we liked best. Pausing a moment to give thanks is a lovely way to begin a meal. We share two graces here from Father John Giuliani of the Benedictine Grange, West Redding, Connecticut (from *One Hundred Graces: Mealtime Blessings*, Bell Tower, 1992):

Bless our hearts
to hear
in the breaking of the bread
the song of the Universe.

God of pilgrims,
give us always a table to stop at
where we can tell our story
and sing our song.

Marcia M. Kelly

BREAKFASTS

Just seven miles from Baltimore, this beautiful, baronial convent and retreat house on eighty-eight acres of wooded land could be in the English countryside. As I looked out to the sunny grounds and rose gardens, one of the nuns told me the following story: She'd been at a wedding in an Episcopal church in the South, where an elderly woman greeted her graciously, and said, "I'm so glad to see a Catholic nun here today." The nun replied, "I'm an Episcopal nun," whereupon the woman dismissed her curtly, saying, "You're wrong, we don't have nuns!"

The nuns are known not just for their delicious food, served in a formal guest dining room in the convent, but also for saving the lives of two newborn bluebirds with broken beaks. The birds soon became part of the community and were often seen perching on Sister Barbara Ann's veil or hiding in her sleeve. A keen observer of nature, she recounts the story in her charming book, *Beakless Bluebirds and Featherless Penguins.*

All Saints Episcopal Convent

Catonsville, Maryland

A HOLIDAY BREAKFAST

•

Breakfast Casserole

Applenola

Pumpkin Bread

Oatmeal Bread

Melt-in-the-Mouth Cookies

From the convent's cookbook *Nun Like It*

BREAKFAST CASSEROLE

•

1 pound sausage

4 slices bread, torn

1 cup grated Cheddar cheese

6 eggs, beaten

2 cups milk

1 teaspoon dry mustard

1 teaspoon salt

Dash pepper

1. Preheat the oven to 350° F.

2. Brown the sausage in a skillet and drain.

3. Layer the bread, sausage, and cheese in a greased 9 × 13-inch baking dish.

4. Combine the remaining ingredients in a bowl and beat well. Pour the mixture over the layers.

5. Bake, uncovered, for 35 to 40 minutes.

SERVES 4 TO 6

APPLENOLA

◆

6 to 12 medium red cooking apples, cored
and cubed but not peeled
¼ cup brown sugar
Ground cinnamon to taste
6 to 8 cups granola
Raisins to taste
Sunflower seeds, shelled
Milk or yogurt

1. Cook the apples overnight in a Crockpot or in the morning in a double boiler. When the apples are tender, add the brown sugar and cinnamon.

2. Add the remaining ingredients as desired.

SERVES 6 TO 8

PUMPKIN BREAD

◆

3½ cups all-purpose flour

2 teaspoons baking soda

½ teaspoon baking powder

1½ teaspoons salt

2 teaspoons pumpkin pie spice

4 eggs

3½ cups sugar

1 cup vegetable oil

2 cups canned or cooked fresh pumpkin

1. Preheat the oven to 350°F.

2. Sift together the flour, baking soda, baking powder, salt, and pumpkin pie spice.

3. Beat the eggs. Add the sugar, the oil, and the pumpkin.

4. Mix the dry ingredients gradually into the mixture. Pour into two 9 × 5 × 3-inch loaf pans and bake for 1 hour.

SERVES 6 TO 8

OATMEAL BREAD

◆

1 cup rolled oats

1 cup scalded milk

3 tablespoons butter

2 teaspoons salt

1 cup cold milk

¾ cup molasses

2 packages dry yeast

½ cup warm water

8 to 10 cups all-purpose flour

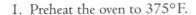

1. Preheat the oven to 375°F.

2. Combine the oats, hot milk, butter, and salt. Stir to melt the butter. Add the cold milk and the molasses. Cool to lukewarm.

3. Combine the yeast and warm (*not* hot) water and allow to stand for 5 minutes.

4. Add the yeast mixture to the oat mixture. Stir in the flour. Knead for 8 to 10 minutes. Let the dough rise in a greased bowl until it has doubled in size. Punch it down and let it rise again. Place in 3 or 4 greased bread pans. Let it rise again.

5. Bake for 25 to 30 minutes, or until done.

SERVES 12 TO 16

MELT-IN-THE-MOUTH COOKIES

♦

½ cup (1 stick) butter, softened

1 cup light brown sugar

1 teaspoon vanilla extract

1 egg

¾ cup all-purpose flour

1 teaspoon baking powder

½ teaspoon salt

½ cup chopped nuts

1. Preheat the oven to 400°F.

2. Cream the butter and sugar. Add the vanilla and egg and beat well. Add the remaining ingredients.

3. Drop by teaspoonfuls onto a greased cookie sheet.

4. Bake for 5 minutes. Let the cookies cool on the pan slightly, until set, before removing.

MAKES 30 COOKIES

This Mennonite retreat, located southwest of Ann Arbor, is approached by a long driveway, looking out to rolling hills. Mennonite craftspeople have rebuilt an old barn with exquisite attention to detail, creating a quiet and restful place. One of the founders says, "Our philosophy is to serve wholesome and nourishing meals. We use little red meat and no canned or packaged soups, cakes, or cookies. We try to make whole-grain bread and serve produce that's in season. We may find fifteen ways of serving zucchini! We make our own salad dressings, yogurt, jams, and jellies and freeze and preserve fruits and vegetables. In winter, we have at least one soup meal each day. In summer, salads are a basic meal." Here they share an unusual breakfast.

A MENNONITE
BREAKFAST

◆

Müsli with bread
and cheese

OR

Overnight Baked
Porridge

Homemade Yogurt

Toasted homemade
bread

juice

MÜSLI

◆

This is a typical main dish in Switzerland, served with bread and cheese. Any of the ingredients can be stretched or omitted.

2 cups yogurt

1 cup rolled oats (quick-cooking)

½ cup flaked coconut

1½ cups canned fruit (peaches, pears, cherries)

1 cup fresh fruit (blueberries, strawberries, peaches, etc.)

¼ cup orange juice

¼ cup honey

½ cup raisins

1. Combine the yogurt, oats, and coconut. Refrigerate for at least 3 hours.

2. Approximately 1 hour before serving, add all the remaining ingredients and chill.

SERVES 4 TO 6

OVERNIGHT BAKED PORRIDGE

◆

3 cups oatmeal

4½ cups boiling water

½ cup oil

1 cup brown sugar

2 eggs, slightly beaten

2 teaspoons baking powder

1 teaspoon salt

¼ teaspoon ground cinnamon

½ cup milk

½ cup raisins

1 apple, peeled, cored, and chopped (optional)

Chopped nuts (optional)

1. Combine the oatmeal and water and allow to stand until the water is absorbed.

2. Add the remaining ingredients.

3. Let the porridge stand overnight in the refrigerator.

4. Bake at 350°F. for 30 minutes. Serve with milk or yogurt.

SERVES 6

HOMEMADE YOGURT

◆

1 *envelope gelatin*

3 *cups cold water plus 2 tablespoons for the gelatin*

1 *cup boiling water*

3 *cups powdered milk*

2 *cups milk, scalded*

1 *8-ounce container nonfat yogurt*

7 *ounces (½ can) sweetened condensed milk*

1. Soften the gelatin in 2 tablespoons of cold water, then dissolve it in 1 cup of boiling water.

2. Stir the powdered milk and remaining cold water together. Add the scalded milk and gelatin water and allow to cool.

3. Mix the yogurt and condensed milk together and add to the mixture.

4. Heat the oven to 250°F. and then turn it off.

5. Put the yogurt in a covered container and place it in the oven for 8 hours. Then put it in the refrigerator, where it will continue to set.

SERVES 6 TO 8

Isis Oasis

Geyserville,
California

A VEGETARIAN
CASSEROLE

◆

Kukuye Sabzi

yogurt and rice

cucumber-and-tomato
salad

pita bread

People often ask which is the most unusual retreat we've ever visited. Isis Oasis, located in a small town eighty miles north of San Francisco, and named after the Egyptian goddess of nature and fertility, is the one that always comes to mind. This eclectic place attempts to bridge the gap between ancient cultures and the New Age and has filled the ten acres beyond the farmhouse with an Egyptian temple, a theater, a collection of exotic birds and animals, and yurts and tepees. An open and spacious dining room serves varied cuisine, including this vegetarian casserole, which can be eaten for breakfast, lunch, or dinner. It is said that this recipe was given to them in Cairo by a mysterious couple dedicated to keeping the ancient traditions alive. I have also included the blessing they use at mealtimes.

KUKUYE SABZI

•

At Isis Oasis they often cook for large groups, so they chop up just enough greens to fit into their large baking trays and add enough eggs to coat and bind the greens. They often serve this with a cucumber-and-tomato salad and pita bread, as well as yogurt and rice, and top it with some cumin and roasted sesame seeds. If you are of a mind to grow some wheat grass, some clippings from this added to the greens would be a wonderful and healthful addition.

2 cups finely chopped leeks

2 cups finely chopped lettuce

2 cups finely chopped spinach

1 cup finely chopped fresh parsley

1 cup finely chopped scallions

2 tablespoons all-purpose flour

1½ teaspoons salt

½ teaspoon pepper

⅓ cup toasted almonds

8 eggs

⅓ cup butter

1. Preheat the oven to 325°F.

2. Put all the chopped vegetables in a bowl. Add the flour, salt, pepper, and almonds, and mix with the greens. Beat the eggs well and add them to the vegetables.

3. Melt the butter in a 9-inch cake pan and pour the vegetables into the pan.

4. Bake for 1 hour, or until the top is brown.

SERVES 6

Let us thank the Goddess
who we appreciate
for all the abundance
that she does create.
For her love, truth, beauty
that we do emulate.
And now let us join
in the sharing of this plate.

New Orleans Zen Temple

New Orleans,
Louisiana

TRADITIONAL ZEN BREAKFAST

♦

*Genmai with
Gomasio*

R obert Livingston, *roshi* and founder of this Zen Buddhist center writes, "At the New Orleans Zen Temple, every morning after *zazen* we eat *genmai*, which has been a traditional breakfast in Zen temples for centuries. It is very balanced and robust and should always be the first meal of your day. It is great for the digestive tract, and along with *zazen*, is excellent in bringing the body-mind back into equilibrium.

"I was introduced to *genmai* at the Paris Zen temple of my master, Taisen Deshimaru, where we served it every morning after *zazen*. Most of Deshimaru's disciples in the Paris *dojo* were French, so after *genmai*, an informal *petit déjeuner* was served—with French baguettes, butter and jam, café au lait, and cigarettes for the smokers (sometimes even whiskey appeared)."

GENMAI

♦

Olive oil

1 cup organic short-grain brown rice

1½ cups spring water

½ teaspoon sea salt

⅓ pound organic carrots

⅓ pound organic celery

⅓ pound organic leeks (or yellow onions)

⅓ pound organic turnips

⅓ pound organic zucchini

*Tamari, toasted sesame salt (gomasio, page 14),
and/or salt*

To prepare the rice:

1. Heat a little good olive oil slightly in the pressure cooker. Put the rice in and stir it for a minute or two in the oil. Add the spring water and the sea salt.

2. Close the cooker and heat on a high flame until the pot starts to hiss. Turn down the heat to low—just hot enough to keep the steam slightly hissing during the cooking—and cook for 45 minutes. Remove the pot from the heat and let it sit for 15 minutes before releasing the steam and opening the pot.

To prepare the vegetables:

3. Wash the vegetables well. Peel the turnips; get all the sand and soil out of the leeks; and scrub the carrots, celery, and zucchini thoroughly. Chop the vegetables as small as possible (the traditional standard is "the size of a grain of cooked rice").

To cook the vegetables:

4. In a large stainless steel pot, heat 1 tablespoon of olive oil and cook the leeks (or onions) slowly until they are translucent. Add the carrots, celery, and turnips along with enough spring water to cover the vegetables—about 3 or 4 inches. Heat and simmer slowly for 45 minutes. Add the zucchini and simmer for another 5 to 10 minutes. The vegetables should be thoroughly cooked.

5. Open the pressure cooker and add the rice to the vegetables. Bring to a simmer, adding a little water if necessary. Stir often with a flat wooden spatula (the *genmai* sticks to the bottom and burns easily) for 20 minutes, until the starch is released from the rice and the *genmai* thickens to the consistency of a heavy soup. Serve with tamari, toasted sesame salt (*gomasio*), and/or salt.

SERVES 6 TO 8

GOMASIO

◆

Prepared *gomasio* is available in health-food stores.

> 7 *teaspoons dark sesame seeds*
> ½ *teaspoon sea salt*

1. Rinse the sesame seeds and toast them in a warm skillet until they pop.

2. Grind the sesame seeds with a mortar and pestle.

3. Heat the sea salt in a dry skillet until it is shiny. Grind and mix the salt with the seeds. This condiment can be saved for future use.

ENOUGH FOR SEVERAL MEALS

Saint Mary's, ninety miles southeast of Nashville, sits on a bluff atop Monteagle Mountain, with glorious views of the mountains beyond. The center hosts groups and individuals, many connected with the University of the South, which is just down the hill. There's a lovely private hermitage on the property, too, along with some rooms in the new monastery. Walking to the chapel through the woods, along the road past grazing cows, to the fishing pond (with poles provided), or playing a round on the university's golf course is perfect preparation for the rich and satisfying food to be found at mealtimes. No holds are barred in the use of butter, cream cheese, and sugar, making for delicious meals from morning to night.

Saint Mary's Episcopal Retreat and Conference Center

Sewanee, Tennessee

A FAVORITE BREAKFAST

•

Cheese Grits

Sour Cream–Cinnamon Breakfast Cake

Fruit and yogurt

CHEESE GRITS

•

    6 *cups water*
    ½ teaspoon salt
    1½ cups uncooked regular grits
    ½ cup (1 stick) butter
    4 cups shredded medium-sharp Cheddar cheese
    3 eggs, beaten

1. Combine the water and salt and bring to a boil. Stir in the grits. Cook until done, following the package directions. Remove from the heat. Add the butter to 3¾ cups of the cheese. Heat, stirring until the cheese melts, then mix into the grits. Add a small amount of the grits to the eggs and stir well.

2. Preheat the oven to 350°F.

3. Add the egg mixture to the hot grits while continuing to stir. Then pour into a lightly greased 2½-quart baking dish. Bake for 10 minutes. Sprinkle with the remaining cheese. Bake for an additional 5 minutes.

SERVES 12

SOUR CREAM–CINNAMON BREAKFAST CAKE

◆

4 eggs

½ cup sugar

Vegetable oil (as much as required
by cake mix directions)

1 package yellow cake mix

1 cup sour cream

¾ cup chopped nuts

¼ cup dark brown sugar

1 tablespoon ground cinnamon

1. Preheat the oven to 350°F.

2. Beat the eggs until thick and fluffy. Add the sugar and oil and beat again.

3. Blend in the cake mix, sour cream, and nuts.

4. Pour half of the batter into a well-greased Bundt pan. Mix the brown sugar and cinnamon and sprinkle over the batter. Swirl in lightly with a knife. Pour the remaining batter on top. Bake for 45 to 50 minutes, until a toothpick comes out clean.

SERVES 12

For meditative inquiry and retreats," reads the sign as you enter this beautiful and remote two hundred acres in western New York. Much of the time here is spent in the meditation hall, whose windows capture the changing light on the hills, fields, and woods beyond. And mealtime, in silence, allows mindful contemplation of the delicious food, with views of clouds and sky through artfully placed skylights and windows. Bowls overflowing with the best oatmeal ever made, with fruits, nuts, yogurt galore, and urns of unique apple-mint tea are a great way to begin the day.

SPRINGWATER CENTER

Springwater, New York

HOT OATMEAL

•

4 cups rolled oats
$\frac{1}{8}$ teaspoon salt
1 tablespoon canola oil
9 cups boiling water
Toasted sesame seeds (optional)

1. Preheat the oven to 275°F.
2. Mix all of the ingredients except the sesame seeds in a Dutch oven and stir.
3. Cover and place in the oven for 20 minutes.
4. Rotate the pot, stir, and lower the heat to 175°F. Cook for 10 minutes, or until you are ready to serve. Serve sprinkled with sesame seeds, if desired.

SERVES 6 TO 8

WINTER BREAKFAST

•

Hot Oatmeal

Homemade Yogurt*

Stewed Prunes and Apricots

warm orange-blossom honey

Fresh Fruit

Apple-Mint Tea

*Thanks to Nadine and Ken Delano

HOMEMADE YOGURT

◆

1 gallon whole or low-fat milk

½ cup yogurt, at room temperature

½ teaspoon yogurt starter

Heat the milk on a medium-high flame until it is 180°F. Combine the yogurt and the yogurt starter, then whip them into the milk and pour into 4 mason jars. Keep warm for 5 to 12 hours in a cooler or over the stove pilot light, then cover and refrigerate.

SERVES 6 TO 8

STEWED PRUNES AND APRICOTS

◆

½ pound each dried prunes and dried apricots

Cinnamon stick or strip sliced lemon or orange peel

1. Cover the prunes and apricots with cold water and bring to a boil. Simmer until they are puffy, about 20 minutes.

2. Add a piece of cinnamon stick. Cook for 10 minutes or more. Let the mixture stand until syrupy.

SERVES 6 TO 8

APPLE-MINT TEA

◆

6 cups apple juice

6 cups mint tea

Orange-blossom honey

1. Mix the juice and tea together and heat.

2. Serve with orange-blossom honey, which can be warmed in the jar in a pot of hot water.

SERVES 6 TO 8

BRUNCHES, LUNCHES, AND DINNERS

Once a winery, the six hundred acres of this Trappist monastery in the northern Sacramento Valley are now prune and walnut orchards, farmed and harvested by the monks to support their community. And, of course, prunes and walnuts often show up in the delicious meals served in the guest refectory. At the appointed hour, the once-empty buffet tables are, it seems, suddenly magically laden with great vegetarian feasts. Included here are some of the monastery's favorite recipes. Guestmaster Brother Laurin says the sweet-and-sour carrots are so good, one can become addicted to them!

CORN CASSEROLE

◆

16 *ounces canned cream-style corn*

16 *ounces canned sweet corn*

4 *eggs, beaten*

1 *cup cornmeal*

1 *garlic clove, minced*

   Canned jalapeño peppers to taste, minced

½ *teaspoon cumin seeds*

⅔ *cup oil*

   Monterey Jack or Colby cheese, shredded, to taste

1. Preheat the oven to 350°F.

2. Mix together the cream-style corn, sweet corn, eggs, cornmeal, garlic, peppers, cumin, and oil.

3. Pour into a greased baking pan and cook for an hour.

4. Top with shredded cheese for the final 5 or 10 minutes.

SERVES 8

Λbbey of
New Clairvaux

Vina,
California

A FARM MONASTERY VEGETARIAN FEAST

◆

Corn Casserole

Oven-Browned Potatoes

Risotto

Brother Gerard's Biscuit Twisters

Sweet-and-Sour Carrot Salad

tossed green salad with pea pods, broccoli florets, baby carrots, and cauliflower

Prune Cake

OVEN-BROWNED POTATOES

♦

8 potatoes

Oil

Salt, pepper, and paprika

1. Preheat the oven to 400°F.

2. Peel the potatoes and cut them into cubes.

3. Boil the potatoes in salted water for 3 minutes.

4. Drain thoroughly and spread in baking pans.

5. Drizzle with oil and season with salt, pepper, and paprika.

6. Bake 15 to 20 minutes, until browned. The potatoes may be stirred to prevent sticking. Add a little more oil if needed.

SERVES 8

RISOTTO

♦

A recipe Father Mark Scott brought back from Rome!

2 cups white rice

2 garlic cloves, minced

¼ pound (1 stick) unsalted butter

½ cup white wine

Salt, white pepper, turmeric, and dried basil to taste

3 cups boiling water

½ cup diced onion

2 cups grated Parmesan cheese

1. Preheat the oven to 350°F.

2. In a roasting pan, sauté the rice and garlic in butter until the rice is clear and begins to brown.

3. Add the wine, salt, pepper, turmeric, and basil and sauté a little longer.

4. Add the boiling water, cover the pan, and place it in the oven. Bake until the liquid is absorbed, about 20 minutes.

5. Lightly sauté the onion.

6. Fluff the cooked rice, then mix in the Parmesan and the onion.

VARIATIONS   To the cooked rice, add finely chopped walnuts or raw vegetables, diced tomatoes, or sautéed mushrooms.

SERVES 8

BROTHER GERARD'S BISCUIT TWISTERS

◆

1 recipe biscuit dough (Gethsemani's Brother Ambrose's
recipe; see page 50)
Garlic powder
Grated Cheddar cheese

1. Make the biscuit dough. After rolling (step 5), sprinkle with garlic powder and grated Cheddar to taste.

2. Instead of cutting into biscuits, slice into 1-inch strips and twist before baking. Bake as directed in step 7. A fabulous invention!

MAKES 12 TO 15 BISCUIT TWISTERS

SWEET-AND-SOUR
CARROT SALAD
◆

2 pounds carrots

1 medium onion

1 medium green bell pepper

1 8-ounce can tomato sauce

1 cup oil

¾ cup cider vinegar

1 cup sugar

1 tablespoon mustard

1 tablespoon Worcestershire sauce

Salt and pepper to taste

1. Peel the carrots and slice them crosswise or put them through the slicer blade of a salad shooter.

2. Cut the onion into quarters and slice.

3. Dice the green pepper.

4. Mix the carrot, onion, and green pepper in a bowl.

5. Blend the remaining ingredients in a blender.

6. Pour the liquid over the vegetables and marinate for 8 hours.

SERVES 8

PRUNE CAKE

♦

⅔ cup (about 6) chopped prunes

1 slice lemon

2 eggs, beaten

⅔ cup vegetable oil

1 cup sugar

1 scant teaspoon baking soda

⅔ cup buttermilk

⅔ teaspoon ground cinnamon

⅔ teaspoon ground nutmeg

⅔ teaspoon ground allspice

⅔ teaspoon vanilla extract

1⅓ cups white cake flour or pastry flour

⅔ cup chopped walnuts

Confectioners' sugar (optional)

1. Preheat the oven to 350°F.

2. Into a small bowl, pour boiling water over the prunes and lemon. Let sit until the prunes are softened, about 20 minutes. Drain.

3. Mix all of the ingredients except the confectioners' sugar together and pour into a greased and floured 8-inch square or round pan.

4. Bake for about 55 minutes. Allow to cool in the pan.

5. Cut into squares and serve plain or dusted with confectioners' sugar.

SERVES 8

Avila Retreat Center

Durham, North Carolina

Named for St. Teresa of Avila, this Catholic retreat center on fifty-one acres in Durham is blessed with a cook named Estella Taylor, a master of Southern cooking. When the meal bells ring, guests come quickly from the lovely cottages scattered throughout the gardens on this lush property. Meals are served in a casual and cheerful dining room decorated with the fine nature photographs taken by the director, Sister Damian Marie Jackson. The adjoining kitchen is always open, so guests can wander in for delicious snacks at any time.

VALENTINE EVENING DINNER

•

Fresh strawberry fruit cup

Estella's Squash Casserole

peas and mushrooms

small green salad

Cheese Biscuits

Bread Pudding with Hard Sauce

From Avila's cookbook, *Sharing Our Best*

ESTELLA'S SQUASH CASSEROLE

•

3 pounds yellow squash

2 large onions, chopped

1 teaspoon salt

$\frac{1}{4}$ teaspoon pepper

3 tablespoons butter (or more)

1 cup bread crumbs

1 cup grated Cheddar cheese

$\frac{1}{2}$ cup milk

1 egg

1. Preheat the oven to 300° F.

2. Cook the squash and onion in boiling water until tender; drain, and mash together.

3. Add the salt, pepper, and butter. Add the bread crumbs and $\frac{1}{2}$ cup of grated cheese. Add the milk and egg. Stir until well blended.

4. Pour into a casserole. Sprinkle with the remaining cheese. Bake for 20 to 30 minutes.

SERVES 8

CHEESE BISCUITS

◆

2 cups vegetable shortening

2 cups grated American cheese

4 cups white flour

1 teaspoon salt

2 teaspoons baking powder

2 cups buttermilk

1. Preheat the oven to 300°F.

2. Combine the shortening, cheese, and flour. Mix thoroughly.

3. Add the salt and baking powder, mix, then add the buttermilk.

4. Knead together and roll out. Cut to desired size.

5. Bake for 7 to 8 minutes.

MAKES 2 DOZEN BISCUITS

BREAD PUDDING
WITH HARD SAUCE

◆

4 eggs

2½ cups sugar

2½ sticks butter

6 cups bread crumbs

2 teaspoons vanilla extract

1 8-ounce can crushed pineapple

1 cup raisins

2 tablespoons ground cinnamon

1½ cups confectioners' sugar

1 teaspoon lemon juice

1 tablespoon water

1. Preheat the oven to 350°F.

2. Beat the eggs and add the sugar.

3. Melt 1½ sticks of butter and add to the crumbs. Stir into the egg mixture.

4. Add the vanilla, crushed pineapple, raisins, and cinnamon and blend together.

5. Place in a 9 × 13-inch baking pan that has been greased or sprayed with nonstick spray.

6. Bake for 1 hour, or until brown.

To make the hard sauce:

7. Mix the confectioners' sugar, lemon juice, and remaining stick of butter with the tablespoon of water (or as much as it takes to make the sauce as thin or as thick as you wish).

8. Serve the bread pudding hot, with the sauce. Mix until smooth with a mixer.

SERVES 8

Silent meals at this Theravadan Buddhist forest meditation center match the simple, contemplative spirit of the place, which seems remote but is only two hours west of Washington, D.C. Food is served in the kitchen, where the monks enter in order of seniority, then return to their places at the benches around the large, plain dining room. Following the Buddha's instructions not to eat after noon, the main meal of the day is taken at 11:15 A.M. This consists of such fare as the hearty soup and homemade wheat bread we include here. Amounts offered are bountiful, since it is the last meal of the day. In winter, there's always a pot of hot water bubbling atop the wood-burning stove so guests can brew one of the many delicious teas offered.

LIMA BEAN SOUP

◆

2 *cups lima beans*

1 *large onion*

3 *stalks celery*

2 *tablespoons olive oil*

1 *tablespoon butter*

¼ *cup chopped fresh dill*

1. Soak the lima beans overnight in water to cover. Drain.

2. Sauté the onion and celery in the olive oil and butter until the onion is transparent.

3. Add the lima beans and water to cover. Cook for about 2 hours.

4. Add the dill ½ hour before serving.

SERVES 6

Bhavana Society

High View, West Virginia

SOUP AND SALAD

◆

Lima Bean Soup

Homemade Wheat Bread

Tossed Salad with Hollyhock Dressing

HOMEMADE WHEAT BREAD

◆

1 tablespoon yeast (or one package)

½ cup tepid water

4 cups whole-wheat flour

2 cups unbleached white flour

1 teaspoon salt

1. Dissolve the yeast in the tepid water. Mix the flours and the salt. Warm in a very low oven, then add to the yeast mixture.

2. Knead for 15 to 20 minutes. Let rise for 1½ hours, then punch down.

3. Let the dough rise again until it doubles in bulk. Form it into one large or two small loaves and allow to rest for ½ hour.

4. Preheat the oven to 350° F.

5. Slash the top of the dough and sprinkle the cuts with water.

6. Bake for 40 to 45 minutes, keeping the loaves covered with an inverted bowl for the first 20 minutes.

MAKES 1 LARGE OR 2 SMALL LOAVES

HOLLYHOCK DRESSING

◆

1 cup balsamic vinegar

1 cup water

1 cup soy sauce or tamari

2 cups olive oil

   Minced fresh garlic to taste

$\frac{1}{2}$ cup chopped fresh basil or parsley

Blend all of the ingredients together. Whatever you don't use
can be stored in a jar in the refrigerator.

MAKES 5 CUPS

Breitenbush Hot Springs

Detroit,
Oregon

A
SOUTHWESTERN
MEAL

◆

Yam-and-Jalapeño
Enchiladas

Tomatillo Sauce

Fresh salsa

organic blue corn chips

Surrounded by the mountains, canyons, cascading streams, and rivers of the Willamette National Forest in northern Oregon, this rustic and beautiful retreat center is famous for its hot springs used by Native Americans for centuries.

I peeked at the minutes of a recent staff meeting posted on a bulletin board in the dining room during our visit. Part of the discussion centered on the continuing effort to make the food not only healthful but delicious. People work up an appetite hiking the trails bordering the Breitenbush River or sitting in one of the several delightful hot springs on the property. The community's concern for good food shows in this original and very popular meal.

YAM-AND-JALAPEÑO ENCHILADAS

◆

1 pound yams, peeled and cut into 1-inch dice
  Olive oil
1 onion, cut into ½-inch dice
1 jalapeño pepper, seeded and minced (be careful when
    chopping not to touch your eyes, and wash your
    hands immediately afterward)
2½ tablespoons sesame seeds
1 tablespoon fresh oregano
¼ pound Monterey Jack cheese, shredded
¼ pound Cheddar cheese, shredded
  Salt and pepper to taste
5 tortillas (corn or wheat)

1 recipe Tomatillo Sauce (see below), heated

    Grated cheese, olives, and chopped scallion for garnish

Fresh salsa

Organic blue corn chips

1. Preheat the oven to 350°F.

2. Place the diced yams on a greased cookie sheet. Brush liberally with olive oil. Bake for 45 minutes, until browned.

3. Meanwhile, sauté the onion and pepper in olive oil, and stir in the sesame seeds and oregano.

4. Toss all of the vegetables together; let cool. Add the cheeses and salt and pepper to taste.

5. Divide the filling equally among the tortillas and roll them up.

6. Pour some of the hot tomatillo sauce into a baking dish, then add the enchiladas. Cover with more sauce and bake for 20 minutes.

7. Sprinkle some cheese, olives, and scallion on top. Broil until the cheese melts. Serve with fresh salsa, organic blue corn chips, and love.

SERVES 4

TOMATILLO SAUCE
◆

3 garlic cloves

1 tablespoon olive oil

2 cups chopped green tomatillo

    Salt and pepper

1 to 2 sprigs fresh cilantro, chopped

Sauté the garlic in olive oil; add the tomatillo, salt, and pepper. Simmer for 20 minutes. Add the cilantro.

SERVES 4

Camp Weed and Cerveny Conference Center

Live Oak,
Florida

.

A PLANTATION PARTY

◆

Low-Country Boil

lots of beer and lemonade

Prepared for the men's retreat of the
Church of the Holy Spirit
on January 14, 1995, by Joe Chamberlain.

Joe Chamberlain, the director of this Episcopal center in northern Florida, insisted on piling us all into his Jeep after dinner one night and driving us by moonlight to the place on the property where he'd cooked this Low-Country Boil. He was particularly proud of the sixty-gallon syrup kettle he'd cooked it in, and which he made us inspect. We include his own personal recipe here. When he's not cooking at this architect-designed, lakeside retreat with its gorgeous new chapel built over the water, two excellent cooks provide a stunning array of choices to the groups who visit.

LOW-COUNTRY BOIL

◆

You begin with a large pot. I chose a 60-gallon syrup kettle. It came from a foundry in Savannah, Georgia. Since there were to be 30 guests, I filled the kettle to about the 30-gallon point—1 gallon per person. Then the water was brought to a boil. To the boiling water I added 4 large onions (chopped), 3 complete bunches of celery (chopped), 15 pounds of smoked link sausage (8 ounces per person), cut in 2-inch lengths, 4 large cans of Old Bay seasoning, a good dash of cayenne pepper, and a handful of salt. Let it boil—about 30 minutes or more won't hurt. Then I added 30 pounds of small new potatoes (1 pound per person) and let them boil until they were half done. At this point I added about 45 fresh ears of Silver Queen corn cut into pieces about 2 inches long. At the point when the corn is almost ready, it's time to add the seafood, so I dropped the following in at the same time: 5 pounds shrimp (about $2\frac{1}{2}$ ounces per person), 30 fresh crawdads (1 per person), and 15 fresh blue crabs (half a crab per person). As soon as the seafood hit the water, it was time to announce that the meal was ready. Any delay would overcook the seafood.

This was the first monastery we ever visited, and we were given the choice, when we called to make our reservation, of staying in the monastery itself or in the guest house on the lake. I opted for the monastery, which meant we had to participate fully in the work, meditation, and dining practices of these Zen Buddhist monks. We even donned monks' robes during our stay. Meals were taken in silence at a long Nakashima-designed table in this breathtakingly beautiful place, high in the Catskill mountains. Anything and everything you put on your plate had to be eaten, which posed quite a problem when the pretty red berries we loaded up on turned out to be "salted plums." No salted plums in this delicious meal though, which, with its subtle spicing and simple ingredients, is still hard to call austere when you're eating it. It allows you to feel great about eating like a spartan.

GINGER RICE

◆

Zen meals are eaten in silence, using a set of three bowls called *jihatsu*. After the meal the monks clean their own bowls so that no time is wasted on extra cleaning up. Naturally, three dishes are prepared. The largest bowl is usually a grain, such as rice, or noodles.

> 2 cups water
>
> 2 tablespoons soy sauce
>
> 2 tablespoons sake *(rice wine)*
>
> 2 inches fresh ginger, peeled and cut into thin strips
>
> 1 cup brown rice

Dai Bosatsu Zendo

Livingston Manor, New York

THREE-BOWL MEAL *JIHATSU*

◆

Ginger Rice

Hot-and-Sour Baked Tofu

Seiko's Noodles with Spinach, Carrots, and Eggs

*First, let us reflect on our own work
and the effort of those who brought
us this food.*

*Secondly, let us be aware of the
quality of our deeds, as we receive
this meal.*

*Thirdly, what is most essential is the
practice of mindfulness, which
helps us transcend greed, anger,
and delusion.*

*Fourthly, we appreciate this food
which sustains the good health of
our body and mind.*

*Fifthly, in order to continue our
practice for all beings we accept
this offering.*

1. Boil the water and add the soy sauce, *sake*, ginger, and brown rice.

2. Bring to a boil again and cover. Reduce the heat and simmer for 45 minutes.

3. Set aside for 10 minutes. Uncover and fluff.

SERVES 4 TO 6

HOT-AND-SOUR BAKED TOFU

◆

1 16-ounce block tofu

4 tablespoons minced fresh ginger

½ cup soy sauce

1 onion, diced

1 small can tomato paste

¼ cup rice vinegar

¼ cup mirin or sake *(rice wine)*

Soy sauce to taste

1 tablespoon minced garlic

Red pepper flakes to taste

1 tablespoon cornstarch

1 tablespoon cold water

1. The day before serving, marinate the tofu by first draining and pressing it to remove the excess water. Chop it into ½-inch cubes.

2. Combine the ginger, soy sauce, and onion, and marinate the tofu in this mixture overnight.

3. Preheat the oven to 400°F.

4. Place the tofu and marinade in an ovenproof casserole. Cover and bake for 40 minutes. Remove from the oven, but leave the oven on.

5. Drain the liquid from the cooked tofu into a bowl and add the tomato paste, rice vinegar, mirin, soy sauce to taste, garlic, and red pepper flakes.

6. Mix the tofu and tomato sauce. Dissolve the cornstarch in the cold water. Pour over the tofu and bake, uncovered, until bubbling, about 20 minutes.

SERVES 4 TO 6

SEIKO'S NOODLES WITH SPINACH, CARROTS, AND EGGS

◆

6 tablespoons minced fresh ginger

4 tablespoons minced garlic

Sesame oil

4 carrots, chopped

1 16-ounce block tofu, chopped

Soy sauce

1 box frozen chopped spinach

4 scrambled eggs

1 package cellophane rice noodles (mei fun),
cooked, rinsed, and chopped

1. Sauté the ginger and garlic in sesame oil in a pan or wok large enough to hold all of the ingredients.

2. Add the chopped carrot and cook over low heat until softened.

3. Add the tofu and soy sauce. Stir.

4. Add the chopped spinach and egg.

5. Add the noodles and toss until hot.

SERVES 4 TO 6

Falkynor Farm

Davie,
Florida

This organic farm outside Fort Lauderdale is run by devotees of Indian guru Sathya Sai Baba. What was once a pasture for Stormy the horse has been transformed into a tropical paradise filled with papayas, bananas, oranges, grapefruit, and exotic flowering plants. The food served reflects the gardens and is beautiful, original, healthful, and simply delicious. Here are two menus, which are sometimes served to students of Falkynor's vegetarian cooking classes, acupressure and other self-health programs, or Thursday night *bhajans* (chanting).

A TROPICAL SUPPER

•

Lime Stew

Green Papaya Coleslaw

Mango Ice Cream

LIME STEW

•

1 medium onion, chopped

2 tablespoons canola oil

7 cups vegetable stock or water

½ cup soy sauce or tamari

4 cups TVP (textured vegetable protein), in rounds or chunks

1 cup lime juice

1 tablespoon vinegar (brown-rice vinegar preferred)

1 cup flour (brown-rice flour preferred)

1 small onion (or 6 scallions), sliced thin

1 medium red bell pepper, sliced thin

1 8-ounce can sliced water chestnuts, drained and rinsed

1 tablespoon toasted sesame oil

2 pounds green beans, cut into 1-inch pieces on the bias

2 pounds yellow summer squash, cut into long thin slivers (not crosswise)

1 pound snow peas, whole or cut into slivers

32 ounces Chinese egg or vermicelli noodles, cooked

1. Sauté the chopped onion in 1 tablespoon of oil until golden brown.

2. Add the stock and soy sauce. Bring to a boil, add the TVP, and simmer for 20 minutes.

3. Add the lime juice and vinegar.

4. Let sit overnight, or for at least 2 hours.

5. Drain the TVP and reserve the liquid. Place the TVP and the flour in a plastic bag and shake to coat, then fry in the remaining tablespoon of oil until golden-brown. Drain well on paper towels.

6. In a large nonstick skillet, sauté the sliced onion, red bell pepper, and water chestnuts in sesame oil until tender.

7. Add the green beans and sauté until almost tender. Stir in the squash and sauté for 3 to 5 minutes. Add the fried TVP and reserved liquid and bring to a boil. Reduce the heat and simmer for 10 to 15 minutes, stirring frequently. Add the snow peas and simmer for 1 to 2 minutes.

8. Serve the stew over the hot noodles.

SERVES 8 TO 10

Green Papaya Coleslaw

◆

2 medium green papayas (about 3 pounds each)

1 small carrot, grated

1 cup canola or soy mayonnaise

½ cup brown-rice vinegar

¼ cup maple syrup

½ teaspoon Herbamare (herbal sea salt) or plain sea salt

1. Remove the seeds from the papayas; peel and grate them.

2. Mix the papaya and carrot.

3. Blend the mayonnaise, vinegar, maple syrup, and Herbamare until smooth.

4. Pour the dressing over the grated papaya and carrot and mix well. Serve chilled.

SERVES 8

VARIATION   Low-fat option: Use low-fat or fat-free mayonnaise, or a vinaigrette slaw dressing.

MANGO ICE CREAM

◆

This can also be served in place of dairy cream over fruit, pies, or grains.

> 4 large ripe mangoes
> 1 pint almond or cashew cream (see below) or coconut
>   cream (can be purchased, frozen, in grocery stores)
> Sprigs of fresh mint

ALMOND CREAM

> ½ cup blanched almonds
> ½ cup water
> 2 pitted dates or dried figs
> ¼ teaspoon frozen orange juice concentrate
> Pinch sea salt

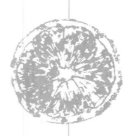

CASHEW CREAM

> ½ cup cashews
> ½ cup water
> 1 tablespoon sweetener (maple syrup, apple-juice
>   concentrate, rice syrup, or 2 pieces dried fruit)
> ¼ teaspoon vanilla extract
> Pinch sea salt

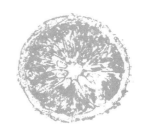

1. The day before serving, peel and slice the mangoes, put them in a plastic bag, and freeze them.

To make the almond or cashew cream:

2. In a food processor or blender, chop the nuts to a fine powder or creamy butter. Add the remaining ingredients and process until smooth. Chill.

3. When ready to serve, place the frozen mango slices in a food processor and blend until creamy. Add the cream; mix well and serve in parfait glasses with a sprig of fresh mint.

SERVES 8

PIZZA PARTY

◆

Tomato-Veggie Pizza

Miso-Veggie Pizza

Potato-Fennel Pizza

Fresh Fruit "Gello"

TOMATO-VEGGIE PIZZA

◆

These pizzas can be served in bite-sized pieces as an appetizer or as a one-dish meal. It is a taste treat when everyone can try each pizza.

CRUST (BUTTERMILK BISCUIT RECIPE)

   1 teaspoon baking soda

   1 tablespoon baking powder

   3 cups all-purpose flour

   1 teaspoon sea salt

   $\frac{1}{4}$ cup melted butter or vegetable oil

   $\frac{3}{4}$ cup buttermilk or almond, coconut, or other nut milk

   1 tablespoon brown-rice vinegar

THE SAUCE

   3 cups thick homemade tomato sauce, unseasoned, or
      1 large can (28 ounces) Progresso Crushed
      Tomatoes with added puree

   Several sprigs each fresh basil, marjoram, oregano,
      parsley, rosemary, and thyme (or $\frac{1}{2}$ teaspoon dried)

   1 teaspoon Herbamare (herbal sea salt) or to taste

   1 tablespoon maple syrup or other natural sweetener

TOPPINGS

   1 head broccoli, cut into bite-sized florets

   1 pound fresh green beans, cut into 1-inch pieces

   2 large red bell peppers, sliced thin

   2 medium onions, sliced thin

   Olive oil

   $\frac{1}{2}$ can black olives, sliced

   1 8-ounce package Almond Rella or Tofu Rella
      mozzarella-style "cheese," grated

To make the crust:

1. Preheat the oven to 350 or 375°F.

2. Sift the baking soda and powder into the flour and salt and mix well.

3. Mix in the butter with a pastry cutter or a large fork. Stir in the buttermilk and the vinegar. Gently mix together into a ball of dough. Then roll out on two large, round, oiled pizza pans or one 12 × 17-inch rectangular baking sheet.

4. Bake for 10 to 15 minutes, or until lightly browned. (Roll thinner and bake longer for crispy crusts.)

To make the sauce:

5. Place the unseasoned sauce or crushed tomatoes in a small saucepan. Chop the fresh herbs and add them to the tomatoes. Add the salt and sweetener. Stir well and simmer on medium heat for about 1 hour.

To prepare the toppings:

6. Steam the broccoli for 5 minutes, or until tender. Steam the green beans for 5 minutes, or until tender.

7. Sauté the red bell pepper and onion in a small amount of olive oil until tender.

8. When the pizza crusts and vegetables are cooked, gently spread the tomato sauce, a little at a time, over the crust. (You will have some sauce left over.)

9. Add the toppings in this order: onion slices, broccoli florets, green beans, red bell pepper slices, and olives. Sprinkle grated cheese over the vegetables and bake for 5 minutes, or until the cheese is melted.

SERVES 6

VARIATION   Add or substitute yellow squash, zucchini, cauliflower, artichoke hearts, or other favorite vegetables.

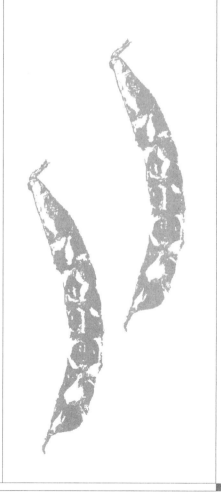

MISO-VEGGIE PIZZA

◆

1 crust (Buttermilk Biscuit Recipe; see page 42)

SAUCE

$1\frac{1}{2}$ cups soy mayonnaise

$\frac{1}{2}$ cup chick-pea miso

$\frac{1}{4}$ cup Braggs Liquid Aminos

1 teaspoon dried basil or 2 teaspoons fresh

$\frac{1}{2}$ cup water

1 teaspoon onion powder

$\frac{1}{4}$ cup maple syrup or other natural sweetener

$\frac{1}{4}$ cup brown-rice vinegar

TOPPINGS

Follow the instructions for Tomato-Veggie Pizza

toppings (page 42)

1. Prepare the crust.

To make the sauce:

2. Place all of the ingredients in a food processor and blend until creamy. (This sauce is also great as a salad dressing or a pasta sauce.)

POTATO-FENNEL PIZZA

◆

1 crust (Buttermilk Biscuit Recipe; see page 42)

SAUCE

5 pounds potatoes, peeled and sliced thin

1 tablespoon butter

1 tablespoon olive oil

4 celery stalks, sliced thin

1 medium onion, sliced thin

½ fennel bulb, sliced thin

1 package (10 ounces) frozen peas

6 sun-dried tomatoes, chopped fine

¼ teaspoon dried chervil or tarragon, or ½ teaspoon fresh

⅛ teaspoon cayenne

¼ teaspoon freshly ground black pepper

2 teaspoons Herbamare (herbal sea salt) or more to taste

¼ cup sherry

Almond Rella or Tofu Rella Cheddar or
mozzarella-style "cheese," grated (optional)

1. Prepare the crust.

To make the sauce:

2. Steam the potato slices for 20 minutes or cook in the pressure cooker for 5 minutes. Set aside to cool, and save the cooking water.

3. Preheat the oven to 350°F.

4. In a large skillet or soup pot, heat the butter and oil. Sauté the celery, onion, and fennel until tender. Add the peas, sun-dried tomatoes, chervil, cayenne, black pepper, Herbamare, sherry, and enough potato water to make a soupy sauce. (The sauce will taste salty, but the potatoes will absorb the excess.)

5. Gently stir in the potato slices, and pour onto the baked pizza crust.

6. Top with grated cheese if desired, and reheat for a few minutes in the preheated oven.

SERVES 6

VARIATION 1   Any soy sausage or meatless burger crumbled or cut in small pieces can be added for a heartier meal.

VARIATION 2   Instead of baking the crusts, then adding the sauce and toppings, try a pizza roll: Roll out the crusts. Add the sauce and a thin layer of the toppings. Carefully fold the crusts from one side of the pan over the fillings to make a long cylindrical pizza roll or calzone. Bake at 350° F. for 30 to 45 minutes, or until golden. Then cut into 4-inch pieces.

FRESH FRUIT "GELLO"

◆

Experiment with your own juice combinations for a different taste.

> ⅓ cup agar-agar flakes
>
> 1 cup orange juice
>
> 1 cup grape juice
>
> 1 cup crushed pineapple with juice
>
> Fresh fruit in season, sliced
>
> Almond or cashew cream (see page 41)

1. In a saucepan, dissolve the agar-agar flakes in the orange and grape juices and bring to a boil.

2. Add the pineapple, reduce the heat, and simmer for about 5 minutes, stirring continuously. Cool, then refrigerate until set.

3. Top with sliced fruit in season and thick almond or cashew cream.

SERVES 4

My life has been intertwined with Gethsemani since early childhood, when Thomas Merton, a close college friend of my uncle, the poet Robert Lax, became a monk of Gethsemani, a Trappist monastery an hour from Louisville, Kentucky. Perhaps this lifetime awareness of monasteries helped lead us on our *Sanctuaries* travels. We'd never known about the food there, until Tommie O'Callaghan, an old friend of the abbey, a trustee of the Merton literary estate, and a caterer, was kind enough to share her experiences in the abbey kitchen, helping Brother Joachim, Brother Ambrose, and the other monks as they took their turns cooking.

Tommie is proudest of teaching them to save all fresh vegetable scraps, onion skins, celery tops, and carrot scrapings to cook down for a residual broth to use as a base for soups, stews, and rice water. The following recipes provide lots of scraps for the pot and delicious eating for monks and guests alike.

Abbey of Gethsemani

Trappist,
Kentucky

A MONK'S MEAL

•

Corn Chowder

Cabbage and Polenta

Brother Ambrose's
Biscuits

CORN CHOWDER

♦

This soup, served with a salad and bread, can make a full meal.

   1 *cup chopped green and red bell pepper*
   1 *cup sliced celery*
   1 *cup chopped onion*
   2 *potatoes, peeled and diced*
      Fresh basil and parsley to taste
   2 *bay leaves*
      Salt and pepper to taste
   1 *teaspoon paprika, cayenne, or Louisiana spice*
   2½ *cups fresh or frozen corn kernels*
   2 *cups milk*
   2 *cups heavy cream*
      Chopped fresh herbs

1. Sauté the bell pepper, celery, and onion until soft and add the diced potato, herbs, salt, pepper, and paprika.

2. Add 3 cups of hot water and cook, covered, over medium heat until the potatoes are barely tender.

3. Puree half the corn and add it to the vegetables. Add the rest of the corn along with the milk and cream.

4. Stir and serve hot. Garnish with chopped fresh herbs.

SERVES 8

CABBAGE AND POLENTA

◆

1 13-ounce box polenta

½ cup olive oil (or a mixture of olive oil and butter, margarine, or vegetable oil)

1 large red onion, chopped

Chopped garlic (optional)

1 cabbage, chopped

4 medium new potatoes, quartered but unpeeled

2 large carrots, chopped into ½-inch-thick slices

1 teaspoon cumin

1 teaspoon salt

1 teaspoon pepper

1½ cups cooked bow-tie or tortellini pasta

¼ cup grated Parmesan cheese

4 tablespoons chopped fresh parsley

1. For the polenta, follow the directions on the package (or the first two steps of the recipe on page 74 or that on page 126). Cook the polenta until it is thick and pour it into a 9 × 12-inch baking pan so that it is about ½ inch thick.

2. Preheat the oven to 350°F.

3. In a large skillet, heat the olive oil until it sizzles and quickly add the onion. (This is a good place to add some chopped garlic, if you wish.) Add the cabbage and cook until it's a bit soft. Add the raw potatoes, carrots, cumin, salt, and pepper. Cover and continue until the carrots and potatoes are al dente.

4. Remove from the heat and stir in the cooked pasta.

5. Ladle onto the polenta base.

6. Sprinkle with cheese and bake until the polenta is hot, about 15 minutes. Decorate with parsley.

SERVES 8

BROTHER AMBROSE'S BISCUITS

◆

1 *package yeast*

1 *cup buttermilk*

2 *cups all-purpose flour*

$\frac{1}{2}$ *teaspoon salt*

$\frac{1}{2}$ *teaspoon baking soda*

1 *tablespoon sugar*

$\frac{1}{2}$ *cup vegetable shortening*

2 *cups shredded Cheddar cheese*

$\frac{1}{2}$ *stick butter, melted*

1. Dissolve the yeast in the buttermilk.

2. Sift the dry ingredients together.

3. Add the shortenings and cheese to the dry ingredients and mix until crumbly.

4. Add the buttermilk and yeast all at once and stir until the dough pulls away from the bowl.

5. Knead by hand for 30 seconds. Roll out $\frac{1}{2}$ to 1 inch thick. Cut into squares or use a cookie cutter.

6. Place on a greased baking sheet and brush with melted butter. Let rise for 1 hour. Meanwhile, preheat the oven to 450° F.

7. Bake for 15 to 20 minutes, or until lightly browned.

MAKES 12 TO 15 BISCUITS

"Would you like me to make you something for dinner?" asked our host, John Paul Weber, as we sat in his beautiful geodesic dome in Wilson Canyon, looking out at the juniper trees and the rugged Arizona foothills beyond. We'd soaked in his tropical tub, surrounded by glorious flowering plants, meditated in the calm of his retreat room, joined by his very mellow cat, and felt we couldn't go wrong accepting this invitation. Soon the smells of curry came our way, and we sat down together to a marvelous Indian feast. John Paul has published a cookbook in the meantime, from which the following meal comes.

ENCHILADA CASSEROLE

•

Canola oil

1 large onion, chopped

1 small green bell pepper, sliced

1 small red bell pepper, sliced

3 garlic cloves, minced or chopped

1 pound zucchini or yellow squash, sliced

1 pound mushrooms, sliced

Basil, oregano, and parsley to taste

2 cups fresh or frozen corn kernels

1 can (15 ounces) enchilada sauce

Corn tortillas (at least 2 dozen)

2 cups grated Cheddar cheese

1 cup chopped olives

The Healing Center of Arizona

Sedona,
Arizona

SUNDAY SUPPER IN ARIZONA

•

Enchilada Casserole

Herbed
Mushroom Rice

Ignacia's Bean Salad

Isleta's Rice Pudding
with Apricots

From John Paul Weber's
The New Gourmet Vegetarian Cookbook

51

1. Heat the oil in a large skillet. Cook the chopped onion, bell peppers, garlic, zucchini, mushrooms, and herbs. Add the corn, cover, and turn the heat down to a simmer.

2. Empty the can of enchilada sauce into a separate large skillet and heat do but not boil.

3. Preheat the oven to 350° F.

4. Pour 1 inch of oil into a small skillet and heat to near high.

5. Using tongs, take a corn tortilla and dip it in the hot oil until it is cooked on both sides but not stiff. Then dip it in the warmed enchilada sauce and place it on the bottom of a large casserole. Repeat until the bottom and sides of the dish are lined with the dipped corn tortillas.

6. Fill with the vegetable mix and then cover the whole dish with more dipped corn tortillas (these can be cooked stiffer in the hot oil), grated cheese, the remainder of the enchilada sauce from the skillet, and the chopped olives.

7. Place in the oven and bake until the cheese melts.

SERVES 8 TO 10

HERBED MUSHROOM RICE
◆

1 pound fresh mushrooms, sliced

½ stick butter or ¼ cup olive oil

2 cups rice

1 quart water

¼ cup miso

2 teaspoons shredded fresh parsley

1 teaspoon fresh chervil or sage, chopped

1 teaspoon sea salt

1. Sauté the mushrooms in the butter until golden.

2. Stir in the rice.

3. Add the water, miso, parsley, chervil, and salt.

4. Cover and simmer for 30 to 35 minutes, or until all the moisture is absorbed and the rice is fluffy.

SERVES 8

IGNACIA'S BEAN SALAD

◆

1 pound (or one 16-ounce can) cooked pinto beans

1 large sweet onion, sliced very thin

2 cups cooked green beans

1 large bell pepper, seeded and shredded

⅓ cup honey

1 teaspoon chili powder

3 teaspoons sea salt

½ cup sunflower seed oil (or other oil)

½ cup mild vinegar

1. Combine the beans, onion, green beans, and bell pepper in a large bowl.

2. In another bowl, combine the honey, chili powder, and sea salt.

3. Pour the honey mixture over the vegetables and drizzle with oil and vinegar. Chill overnight.

SERVES 8

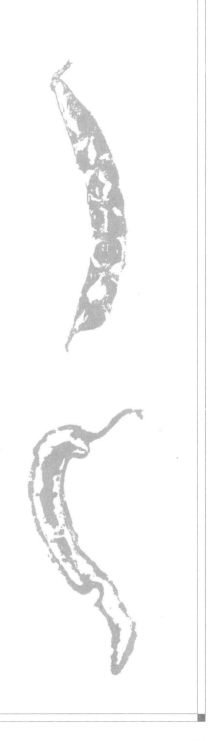

Isleta's Rice Pudding with Apricots

◆

½ cup rice

2 quarts milk

1 teaspoon ground cinnamon

1 cup dried apricots, soaked

1 tablespoon honey

1 teaspoon sea salt

4 eggs

1. Preheat the oven to 275°F.

2. Wash the rice and add the milk, cinnamon, apricots, honey, and sea salt.

3. Separate the eggs. Beat the whites until very stiff. Add the beaten yolks, and fold into the rice mixture.

4. Spoon into a casserole.

5. Bake for 2 hours, stirring several times.

SERVES 8

An elegant, well-dressed woman greeted us as we entered the door of this lakeside monastery adjoining the campus of St. Leo College, an hour north of Tampa. It turned out she was Sister Irma Multer, who was to be our guide and helper throughout our stay. And she had a fantastic story to tell: When she was just out of high school in a small Texas town some sixty years ago, a family member asked her to deliver a package to some local nuns. She did so that evening on her way to a dance, one of her favorite pastimes. The nuns were packing, and this pretty teenager asked where they were going. "To Florida," they replied, and young Irma responded, "I'm going with you." She went on to the dance and told her friends her amazing decision. Three of them spontaneously said they'd go too, and they did. Three of these lovely women, now in their eighties, still live serenely at this lakeside monastery they joined all those years ago.

It's a lively and friendly community, and dinnertime allows everyone to share the stories of their varied days out in the world. We dined on tasty, home-cooked food at a table with a nun who rides her motorcycle to work at the college each day, a man from Massachusetts who volunteers to help with their Elderhostels each year, and a sister on sabbatical. After dinner all don aprons and cheerfully do the dishes together. Here is their Traditional New Year's Dinner.

Holy Name Monastery

St. Leo,
Florida

TRADITIONAL NEW YEAR'S DINNER

•

Baked Ham with Orange Glaze

Black-eyed Peas

Sweet Potatoes

Collard Greens

Cucumber-and-Tomato Salad with Cream Dressing

Corn Bread

Southern Pecan Pie

Baked Ham with Orange Glaze

◆

2 to 3 pounds cooked ham

1 cup brown sugar

Juice and grated rind of 1 orange

½ cup orange marmalade

Cloves

1. Let the ham come to room temperature and bake according to the directions given by the packer or in a slow (300° F.) oven until within 45 minutes of the total baking time. Remove from the oven and increase the temperature to 325° F.

2. Remove the rind from the ham. Make a series of shallow cuts across the fat in square or diamond patterns.

3. Mix the brown sugar, orange juice and rind, and marmalade.

4. Spread the orange glaze over the ham and insert 1 clove into each square of fat.

5. Bake 45 minutes.

SERVES 6 TO 8

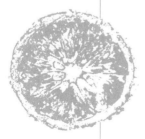

BLACK-EYED PEAS

◆

1 1-pound bag dried black-eyed peas

1 ham hock or hog jowl

1 medium-sized onion, chopped

   Salt and pepper to taste

1. Wash the peas and soak them overnight in approximately 4 times as much water.

2. Add the ham hock or hog jowl to the peas and soaking water. Bring to a vigorous boil, stirring often, then reduce to a simmer.

3. Add the onion.

4. Cook for 1½ to 2 hours. When three-quarters done, add salt and pepper to taste.

SERVES 6 TO 8

SWEET POTATOES

◆

12 sweet potatoes or yams

    Butter

1. Preheat the oven to 450°F.

2. Scrub the potatoes.

3. Place them in a baking pan or on the oven rack. Bake until tender, about 40 minutes. (To test the potatoes, squeeze them. When they are soft, break the skins to keep them from getting soggy.)

4. Serve with plenty of butter.

SERVES 12

COLLARD GREENS

◆

2 *pounds collard greens*

1 *small onion, chopped*

1 *chicken bouillon cube*

1 *tablespoon butter*

Salt

1. Wash the collard greens thoroughly. Tear or cut the leaves into narrow strips. Place them in a pot and almost cover them with water.

2. Add the onion, chicken bouillon cube, and butter.

3. Salt to taste, bring to a boil, and cook until tender, 20 to 30 minutes after the water has boiled.

SERVES 6 TO 8

CUCUMBER-AND-TOMATO SALAD WITH CREAM DRESSING

◆

4 *cucumbers, peeled and sliced very thin*

Salt

4 *tablespoons vinegar*

4 *tablespoons sugar*

2 *cups heavy cream, whipped*

4 *tomatoes, sliced*

1. Sprinkle the cucumbers with a little salt and let them stand for 15 minutes.

To make the dressing:

2. Combine the vinegar, sugar, and cream.

3. Fold the cucumbers and tomatoes into the dressing.

SERVES 6 TO 8

CORN BREAD

◆

$1\frac{1}{2}$ cups milk, scalded

$1\frac{1}{2}$ cups white cornmeal

1 teaspoon salt

2 tablespoons vegetable shortening

$2\frac{1}{2}$ teaspoons baking powder

1 egg, separated

4 strips bacon, cooked and diced

1. Preheat the oven to 400°F.

2. Mix the milk with the cornmeal and stir in the salt and shortening. Cool.

3. Add the baking powder and egg yolk and mix well.

4. Beat the egg white until stiff. Fold into the batter.

5. Pour into a greased 8 × 8- or 7 × 9-inch pan, sprinkle with diced bacon, and bake for 20 minutes. Serve warm, with honey or molasses.

MAKES ONE LOAF;
SERVES 6 TO 8

SOUTHERN PECAN PIE

◆

1 cup sugar

4 tablespoons all-purpose flour

1/2 teaspoon salt

3 eggs

2 tablespoons water

1 cup white corn syrup

1 teaspoon vanilla extract

1 cup pecans

2 tablespoons butter, melted

1 unbaked pie shell

1. Preheat the oven to 425°F.

2. Mix the sugar, flour, and salt.

3. In a separate bowl, beat the eggs with the water. Fold in the syrup and vanilla, and add to the flour mixture.

4. Mix the pecans and the butter and add to the mixture.

5. Pour into the unbaked pie shell. Bake for 10 minutes. Reduce the heat to 350°F. and bake for another 25 to 30 minutes.

SERVES 6 TO 8

This large stone manor house on twenty-six acres of beautiful grounds is inviting in every way. When the sun streams in the windows of the lovely bedrooms in the morning, you know that members of this community of former nuns are picking oranges from their own trees to squeeze juice for breakfast; you know that after a day wandering in the gardens or reading in the library, there will be tea and homemade chocolate chip cookies waiting for you in the kitchen; and you come to look forward to a dinner around the large table in the gracious dining room with the guests and community. A relaxed atmosphere pervades, and after the last delicious bite, it's fitting to saunter up to the small chapel for a brief nondenominational evening prayer and thanks.

CELEBRATION SPAGHETTI

•

1 tablespoon olive oil

2 medium zucchini, sliced

2 cups sliced mushrooms

1 medium green bell pepper, sliced

1 cup canned black olives, sliced

1 28-ounce can tomatoes, broken up

2 6-ounce cans tomato paste

¼ cup grated cheese of choice

1 teaspoon salt

½ teaspoon dried basil

¼ teaspoon pepper

1 pound spaghetti

2 tablespoons margarine, softened

Grated Parmesan cheese

Immaculate Heart Community

Santa Barbara,
California

COMMUNITY SUPPER

•

Celebration Spaghetti

Chinese Coleslaw

Chocolate Chip Cookies

1. Heat the oil in a large skillet. Sauté the zucchini, mushrooms, green bell pepper, and olives.

2. Add the tomatoes, tomato paste, cheese, salt, basil, and pepper. Simmer for 15 minutes. (If necessary, add boiling water to thin out the tomato paste.)

3. Cook and drain the spaghetti. Toss with the softened margarine.

4. Pour the sauce over the pasta and top with grated Parmesan.

SERVES 8 TO 10

CHINESE COLESLAW
◆

$\frac{1}{4}$ cup rice wine vinegar

$\frac{1}{4}$ to $\frac{1}{3}$ cup sugar

2 tablespoons soy sauce

$\frac{1}{2}$ cup oil

2 packages ramen noodles (discard seasoning)

$\frac{1}{2}$ cup sesame seeds

$\frac{1}{2}$ cup sunflower seeds

2 tablespoons margarine

1 head Napa or Chinese cabbage, chopped

1 bunch scallions, sliced

1. To make the dressing: Combine the vinegar, sugar, soy sauce, and oil. Set aside.

2. Brown the noodles, sesame seeds, and sunflower seeds in margarine.

3. Mix with the cabbage, scallions, and dressing.

4. Bring to a boil and simmer for 1 minute, stirring constantly. Cool before serving but do not serve cold.

SERVES 8 TO 10

CHOCOLATE CHIP COOKIES

◆

2¼ cups all-purpose flour

1 teaspoon baking soda

1 teaspoon salt

1 cup (2 sticks) butter, softened

¾ cup white sugar

¾ cup brown sugar

1 teaspoon vanilla extract

2 eggs

1 cup chopped walnuts

1 12-ounce package semisweet chocolate morsels

1. Preheat the oven to 375°F.

2. Combine the flour, baking soda, and salt in a small bowl.

3. Beat the butter, sugars, and vanilla in a large bowl. Beat in the eggs. Gradually fold in the flour mixture. Stir in the nuts and chocolate.

4. Drop by rounded tablespoons onto ungreased baking sheets. Bake for 10 to 12 minutes.

MAKES 2 DOZEN COOKIES

Insight Meditation Society

Barre,
Massachusetts

SILENT RETREAT SUPPER

•

Mushroom-Almond-
Rice Casserole

Baked Carrots and
Parsnips

Steamed Kale

Green Salad

Beyond Greens
Dressing

Pears with Raisin Sauce

Afriend who regularly attends the Vipassana silent retreats at this Buddhist center said she finds nothing as blissful as sitting in the meditation hall filled with one hundred silent retreatants. "You feel a oneness with others, a feeling of pure love." Year after year, all the spaces are filled for the three-month silent retreat at this Georgian brick mansion near Worcester—an indication of our yearning for something beyond our busy lives. It's a reflection of the practice of mindfulness taught here that the cooks continue to produce delicious and healthful meals. At each meal you can observe the silent diners with smiles on their faces. Try the following recipes and you'll discover why.

MUSHROOM-ALMOND-RICE CASSEROLE

•

2 tablespoons canola oil

1 large onion, diced

2 stalks celery, diced

1½ cups sliced mushrooms

1 teaspoon each dried marjoram, basil, thyme, and sage

1 teaspoon sea salt (or to taste)

2 cups raw brown rice, cooked in 4½ cups water

½ cup almonds, toasted and coarsely ground

¼ cup sunflower seeds, toasted and coarsely ground
    Freshly ground black pepper to taste

½ to 1 pound tofu, crumbled, or ⅓ cup grated Cheddar
    cheese (both optional for a heartier dish)

1 cup vegetable broth

1. Preheat the oven to 350°F.

2. Heat the oil in a skillet. Sauté the onion until translucent; add the celery and mushrooms, and cook until the mushrooms release their water. Add the herbs and salt and sauté for a few more minutes.

3. In a large bowl, add the vegetables to the cooked rice. Add the ground nuts and seeds, pepper, tofu, if included, and vegetable broth; mix well. Spread the mixture into an oiled casserole, sprinkle cheese on top, if included, cover, and bake for 30 to 45 minutes.

SERVES 4

BAKED CARROTS AND PARSNIPS

◆

½ pound carrots

½ pound parsnips

2 to 3 tablespoons canola oil, plus some for pan

1 tablespoon lemon grass (or dried herbs of choice)

1. Preheat the oven to 275°F.

2. At IMS the cooks tend not to peel vegetables, so wash them all carefully, then chop them into bite-sized pieces of whatever shape you like. IMS cooks often make simple, round slices.

3. Pour the oil over the vegetables, add the lemon grass, and mix with a spoon or with your hands until everything is lightly oiled.

4. Spread evenly across a well-oiled baking sheet and bake for a good hour.

SERVES 4

STEAMED KALE

◆

2 small bunches kale

Wash, chop, and steam the kale. Kale is delightful with just about anything—a robust green. Be sure not to overcook it; it should still have some life (shape and bounce) and color (dark, strong green) to it.

SERVES 4

GREEN SALAD

◆

Lettuce

Grated carrot

Shredded cabbage

Home-grown sprouts

The usual green salad at Insight Meditation Society is simply lettuce with grated carrot and possibly shredded cabbage (purple makes a brilliant color contrast), with an assortment of home-grown sprouts on the side.

BEYOND GREENS DRESSING

◆

2½ cups chopped fresh spinach

2 lemons, peeled, seeded, and cut into small pieces

4 garlic cloves, minced

5 tablespoons tamari

2½ teaspoons dried oregano or 7½ tablespoons fresh

2½ teaspoons dried basil or 7½ tablespoons fresh

2½ cups canola oil

Salt to taste

Blend everything together. Keep the excess in the refrigerator.

MAKES ALMOST A QUART

PEARS WITH RAISIN SAUCE

◆

3 to 4 unripe pears, cut into ¾-inch cubes

Cinnamon sticks

½ cup raisins

1 tablespoon arrowroot

I. Put the chopped pear in a pot with a few cinnamon sticks. Add a little water, bring to a boil, then simmer for a good hour.

To make the raisin sauce:

2. Cover the raisins with water and cook them over medium heat for about 5 minutes. Later, dissolve the arrowroot in a couple of tablespoons of cold water and add to the raisins; cook for a few minutes, until the sauce thickens.

SERVES 4

67

Mepkin Abbey

Moncks Corner,
South Carolina

A MONK'S FEAST

•

Frittata with salsa

Garden Corn Salad

Green Salad with
Father Aelred's
Mother's Dressing

Sun-dried Tomato
Pesto with Pasta

Corn Bread Casserole

Brother Boniface's
French Bread

The noon meal at this lovely plantation on the Cooper River near Charleston, which was once owned by Clare Booth Luce, is always an adventure. The dining rooms of the guests and the Trappist monks adjoin each other, and for the main meal of the day, the two groups walk together in a buffet line. Every day a different monk is in charge of the meal. When we were there, the food was consistently delicious and plentiful. After filling our plates, we returned to our side of the dining room to eat in silence while a monk read aloud. They were reading Kathleen Norris's *Dakota* during our stay, transporting us to the monasteries of the Dakotas through her eyes, as we happily dined.

FRITTATA

•

1 small onion, chopped

4 tablespoons (½ stick) butter

1 cup small whole mushrooms

1 cup chopped red, green, and yellow bell peppers

12 eggs

⅓ cup sour cream

½ teaspoon ground cumin

½ teaspoon dried thyme

   Black pepper to taste

¼ cup milk, beaten until airy

   Salsa

1. Preheat the oven to 325°F.

2. Sauté the onion in butter. Add the mushrooms and bell peppers. Beat the eggs; add the sour cream, cumin, thyme, pepper, and milk. Pour them into the pan and allow the frittata to sit until the bottom is firm.

3. Remove from the burner, cover, and bake for ½ hour. Serve with salsa.

SERVES 8

Garden Corn Salad

◆

8 ears fresh corn, cooked, chilled, and kernels removed

1 small zucchini, cut into ¼-inch slices

1 large green or red bell pepper, diced

½ cup chopped red onion

16 sweet gherkins, minced

1 cup chopped fresh basil and 8 basil leaves for garnish

½ cup mayonnaise or yogurt

⅓ cup vegetable broth, cooled

¼ cup sour cream or yogurt

Salt and pepper to taste

1. Mix the corn, zucchini, bell pepper, onion, gherkins, and basil.

2. Add the mayonnaise, vegetable broth, sour cream, and salt and pepper to taste.

SERVES 6 TO 8

MEPKIN ABBEY BLESSING

Cantor: *Blessed are they*
who shall feast
in the Kingdom of God.

All: *Blessed are they*
who shall feast
in the Kingdom of God.

Our Father, who art in heaven,
Hallowed be Thy name
Thy Kingdom come,
Thy will be done,
On earth as it is in heaven.
Give us this day our daily bread,
O Father in heaven,
and grant that we
who are filled with good things
from Thy open hand,
may never close our hearts
to the hungry, the homeless,
and the poor.

GREEN SALAD WITH FATHER AELRED'S MOTHER'S DRESSING

◆

¾ cup olive oil

⅓ cup cider vinegar

⅓ cup skinned, cored, and minced fresh tomato

Sugar to taste

Mixed lettuces and young broccoli leaves

1. To make the dressing: Blend the oil, vinegar, tomato, and sugar.

2. Serve on mixed lettuces and young broccoli leaves.

SERVES 6 TO 8

SUN-DRIED TOMATO PESTO WITH PASTA

◆

3 cups sun-dried tomatoes

1½ cups olive oil

1 cup plus 2 tablespoons grated Parmesan cheese

¾ cup walnuts

½ packed cup fresh parsley

3 garlic cloves

2 pounds cooked pasta

Parmesan

Black pepper

1. Blend the tomatoes, olive oil, Parmesan, walnuts, parsley, and garlic in a food processor. Add water if the consistency is too thick.

2. Serve with your hot cooked pasta of choice. Dust with Parmesan and black pepper.

SERVES 8

CORN BREAD CASSEROLE

◆

1 cup yellow cornmeal

1½ teaspoons baking powder

¾ teaspoon salt

2 eggs, lightly beaten

¾ cup sour cream

½ cup canola or other vegetable oil

1 8¾-ounce can corn niblets, drained

1 cup grated Cheddar cheese

2 to 3 tablespoons jalapeño peppers, seeds and ribs removed, or canned green chilies, chopped

Chili powder

1. Preheat the oven to 375° F. Grease a 9-inch square metal pan or a 10-inch cast-iron skillet and place in the oven.

2. In a large bowl, combine the cornmeal, baking powder, and salt.

3. Add the eggs, sour cream, and oil and blend. Stir in the corn.

4. Pour half the batter into the heated pan and cover with the cheese and peppers.

5. Spoon the rest of the batter on top, then sprinkle with chili powder.

6. Bake for 25 to 30 minutes, or until lightly browned. Cut into squares or wedges.

SERVES 6 TO 8

BROTHER BONIFACE'S FRENCH BREAD

◆

5 cups all-purpose flour

2 teaspoons sugar

2 teaspoons salt

1 ounce yeast

1 tablespoon unsalted butter, softened

1¾ cups lukewarm water

Cornmeal

1 egg white

Sesame or poppy seeds

1. In the bowl of an electric mixer, combine 1½ cups of flour, the sugar, salt, undissolved yeast, and butter. Gradually add the water and beat for 2 minutes at medium speed.

2. Add the rest of the flour, or enough to make a thick batter. Beat at high speed for 2 minutes to make a soft dough. Knead for 8 minutes by hand. Put into a greased bowl and let double.

3. Preheat the oven to 375°F. Grease 2 baking sheets and sprinkle them with cornmeal. Roll the dough into 3 or 4 oblong strips (or make thinner strips and braid them) and place them on the baking sheets.

4. Bake for 30 to 40 minutes, or until brown. Halfway through the baking, brush with egg white and sprinkle with sesame or poppy seeds.

MAKES 3 TO 4 LOAVES

My memory of dining at Pendle Hill, the Quaker center outside Philadelphia, is the sound of voices singing together in the kitchen over dishwashing. And this happy spirit is carried into the food preparation and presentation. They serve vegetarian and nonvegetarian food, and it's hot, plentiful, and delicious. Here is an example of each. Guests and community at this vibrant place dine together at long tables in the dining room, where there's much discussion and laughter as the food is shared.

Pendle Hill

Wallingford, Pennsylvania

CAROL RYAN'S BAKED ITALIAN VEGETABLE CASSEROLE WITH POLENTA

◆

A QUAKER EARLY AUTUMN MENU

◆

Carol Ryan's Baked Italian Vegetable Casserole with Polenta

Pendle Hill Bread

Green Salad with Balsamic Garlic Vinaigrette

POLENTA

6 *cups water*

2 *tablespoons butter*

1 *teaspoon salt*

1 *teaspoon freshly ground black pepper*

2 *cups cornmeal*

1 *cup grated Parmesan cheese*

VEGETABLES

2 *tablespoons olive oil*

2 *cups chopped onion*

3 *garlic cloves, crushed*

2 *cups chopped red and green bell pepper*

2 *cups chopped zucchini*

2 *cups chopped eggplant*

3 cups chopped tomato

1 teaspoon chopped fresh parsley

1 teaspoon salt

1 teaspoon freshly ground black pepper

2 cups chopped mozzarella cheese (or equal parts
  provolone and Parmesan)

1. Preheat the oven to 350° F.

To make the polenta:

2. In a heavy pot, bring the water to a boil. Add the butter, salt, and freshly ground black pepper. Reduce the heat to a simmer and gradually stir in the cornmeal. Cook, stirring continuously, for 10 to 15 minutes. Add the Parmesan. Continue to cook until the cornmeal is thick and slides easily from the sides of the pot. Transfer the polenta to a 6-cup high-sided casserole dish.

To prepare the vegetables:

3. Heat the olive oil in a large skillet. Add the onion and garlic. Cook until the onion is soft. Add the bell pepper. Cook for about 3 minutes over medium heat. Add the zucchini and eggplant. Cook, stirring often, for 3 to 5 minutes. Add the tomato (include any juice there is). Cook over medium to high heat, stirring and breaking up the tomato. Add the parsley, salt, and pepper. Reduce the heat to low, cover, and simmer for 15 to 20 minutes.

4. Add the cooked vegetables to the polenta in the casserole. Top with the cheese. Bake for about 20 minutes, or until bubbly and golden on top.

SERVES 8

PENDLE HILL BREAD

◆

Bread baking is an easily acquired skill, but it may take two or three tries before you get it right. Don't get discouraged. Pendle Hill has taught hundreds of folks to make bread, and you'll catch on. Then it's great fun.

2½ cups warm water

2 tablespoons yeast

2 tablespoons molasses

6 cups whole-wheat flour, plus more as needed

1 tablespoon salt

2 tablespoons oil

1. Pour the water into a large mixing bowl. Sprinkle in the yeast and whisk to dissolve. Stir in the molasses and let this mixture sit for a few minutes, until you see the yeast beginning to "work."

2. When the yeast begins to foam and bubble, gradually stir in 1 cup of flour. Beat until the flour is incorporated into the liquid. Do the same with 2 more cups of flour. Mix this batter well—about thirty strokes if by hand, 1 to 2 minutes in a mixer. (You can also use a food processor.) This is called the sponge.

3. Let the sponge rise until it has doubled in size. This takes about 1 hour in a home kitchen—a little less if the kitchen is especially warm.

4. Add the salt, oil, and 3 or so more cups of the flour—until you have a soft, workable dough. Shape into a ball and let rest for 5 to 10 minutes.

5. Divide the ball into 2 pieces. Shape each half into a loaf and place in a greased bread pan. Let rise again until doubled in size. (This takes another ½ hour or so.) Meanwhile, preheat the oven to 350°F.

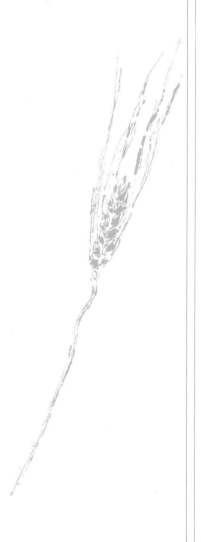

6. Bake for 35 to 45 minutes. Fully baked loaves of bread should leave the pans easily and be an even golden-brown. The bottoms will sound hollow when lightly tapped.

MAKES 2 LOAVES

Green Salad with Balsamic Garlic Vinaigrette

◆

Green salad of your choice

½ cup balsamic vinegar

3 garlic cloves, minced

1½ cups olive oil

1. Prepare the greens.

To make the vinaigrette:

2. Mix the vinegar and garlic in a food processor or with a whisk. Then *slowly* whisk in the olive oil. (You can use less to reduce fat.) The more thoroughly you mix the oil into the vinegar, the better it will emulsify, and the less likely it will be to separate when you store it.

3. Serve with the green salad.

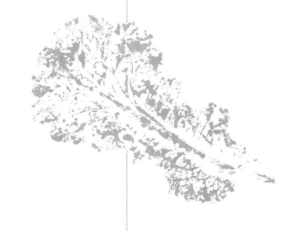

TINA TAU'S CHICKEN WITH ORANGE AND WALNUTS

◆

3 pounds mixed chicken pieces

6 ounces orange juice concentrate

1½ cups coarsely chopped walnuts

Sliced orange (for garnish)

Fresh parsley sprig (for garnish)

1. Preheat the oven to 350° F.

2. Wash the chicken pieces and pat them dry. You can remove the skin and visible fat, as the sauce will keep the pieces moist.

3. Place the chicken pieces on an oiled baking dish and brush liberally with orange juice concentrate.

4. Bake for about 1 hour, basting occasionally with a little more of the concentrate.

5. About 10 minutes before the chicken has finished cooking, sprinkle the chopped walnuts over it. Garnish before serving with sliced orange and a sprig of fresh parsley.

SERVES 8

BAKED YAMS

◆

8 yams or sweet potatoes

Oil

1. Preheat the oven to 400° F.

2. Lightly oil the yams and bake for about 1½ hours.

SERVES 8

A QUAKER SUMMER MENU

◆

Tina Tau's Chicken with Orange and Walnuts

Baked Yams

Steamed Fresh Green Beans

Pendle Hill Cheese Pie

STEAMED FRESH GREEN BEANS

◆

2 pounds fresh green beans

Vinegar

Cook the beans in a steamer. They are fine just as they are, or you can drizzle a little vinegar (or Balsamic Garlic Vinaigrette; see page 76) over them just before serving.

SERVES 8

Like most people, cooks at Pendle Hill use some frozen vegetables in the winter but prefer fresh vegetables when they are available. Fresh vegetables are easy to steam and can be made flavorful without salt by adding herbs to the steaming water. Think of other vegetables: zucchini, yellow squash, and of adding flavorings such as peppers and poppyseed. When was the last time you tasted fresh brussels sprouts? Or try herbed carrots. Slice the carrots very thin, steam for a minute or so, then sauté very lightly in butter and basil.

PENDLE HILL CHEESE PIE

◆

1 pound cream cheese, softened

⅔ cup plus 3 tablespoons sugar

Salt

3 eggs

½ teaspoon almond extract

1 cup sour cream

1 teaspoon vanilla extract

1. Preheat the oven to 350°F.

2. Beat the cream cheese until it is fluffy. Gradually beat in ⅔ cup of sugar and a dash of salt. Add the eggs one at a time, beating after each addition. Continue beating until smooth, then add the almond extract. Pour into a greased 9-inch pie pan and bake for 25 minutes. Remove from the oven and allow to cool away from draughts for 20 minutes. Leave the oven on.

3. While it is cooking, beat together the sour cream, the 3 tablespoons of sugar, a dash of salt, and the vanilla extract. Pour over the pie and bake for 10 more minutes. Cool before eating.

SERVES 8

We came to this Benedictine abbey and private preparatory school by chance one November day when we glimpsed its sign and impulsively turned into the grounds. It was Thanksgiving vacation and the campus was deserted, except for one lone monk carrying a fruitcake under his arm. He invited us on a tour, to join the monks for vespers in their gorgeous chapel, and then on to dinner. Since dinner was in the school dining room, our expectations were not high, so we were particularly delighted at the feast spread out before us on the buffet. Our lone monk has now become the abbot and has shared some of the abbey's favorite recipes with us.

CLAM CHOWDER
•

5 ounces salt pork, diced

1 small onion, chopped fine

½ cup diced celery

3 medium potatoes, peeled and chopped

1 cup clam broth

2 cups water

¼ teaspoon ground thyme

Salt

Black pepper

2½ cups milk

2 cups light cream

4 dozen large clams

1. In a large soup kettle, brown the salt pork and discard. In the rendered fat, sauté the onion and celery until tender.

2. Add the potato, clam broth, water, thyme, and salt and pepper to taste.

3. Simmer, uncovered, until the potato is tender.

4. Stir in the milk, cream, and clams. Heat through, but do not boil.

SERVES 6

MUSHROOMS À LA GRECQUE

♦

½ *cup fresh lemon juice*

½ *cup olive oil*

2 *garlic cloves, peeled and halved*

1 *teaspoon sugar*

1 *teaspoon salt*

1 *teaspoon dried basil*

1 *bay leaf*

¼ *teaspoon black pepper*

2 *large green bell peppers, diced*

1 *onion, diced*

1 *pound small mushrooms, well cleaned but left whole*

2 *medium tomatoes, peeled and chopped*

1. In a saucepan, bring the lemon juice, olive oil, garlic, sugar, salt, basil, bay leaf, and black pepper to a boil. Remove from the heat and cool for 10 minutes.

2. Pour the mixture over the vegetables.

3. Cover and refrigerate overnight, stirring several times. Remove the garlic and bay leaf before serving.

SERVES 6

ROAST DUCKLING À L'ORANGE

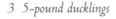

3 5-pound ducklings

1 teaspoon seasoned salt

1/2 teaspoon dried rosemary

1/2 cup chopped celery

1/2 cup chopped onion

2 cups chicken stock

1 tablespoon butter

1/2 cup vinegar

3 tablespoons sugar

1 cup orange juice

1 teaspoon English mustard

1/2 teaspoon cornstarch

1/4 cup Grand Marnier

1. Preheat the oven to 450°F.

2. Trim the ducklings of excess fat at the base of the tails. Rub the insides with the seasoned salt and rosemary. Place the ducklings in a roasting pan, add 1/2 cup of water, and roast for 1 1/2 hours, basting occasionally. Remove the ducklings from the oven and keep warm.

3. Pour off all but 2 tablespoons of fat from the roasting pan. Add the celery and onion, and sauté until tender. Add the chicken stock and simmer for 20 minutes. The basic sauce is now ready for additional flavoring.

4. Melt the butter, vinegar, and sugar in a saucepan and boil until the liquid caramelizes. Add this and the orange juice and mustard to the sauce in the pan and bring to a boil. Strain the sauce, then thicken with cornstarch and season with Grand Marnier. Serve in a warmed sauceboat.

SERVES 6 TO 8

ROAST LEG OF LAMB

◆

1 5-pound leg of lamb

3 garlic cloves, sliced

⅓ cup olive oil

1½ teaspoons oil

Salt to taste

½ teaspoon freshly ground black pepper

1 teaspoon dried rosemary

½ teaspoon dried thyme

½ teaspoon dried sage

Gravy and/or mint jelly, for serving

1. Trim the lamb of fat. Cut slits about ½ inch deep all over the lamb and insert slivers of garlic. Rub all over with olive oil.

2. Combine the salt, pepper, and herbs and rub all over the lamb. Allow to sit at room temperature for 20 minutes. Meanwhile, preheat the oven to 450°F.

3. Roast the lamb for 15 minutes, then turn the oven down to 350°F. Continue to roast until the desired degree of doneness is reached, about an hour for medium-rare. Baste with pan juices once or twice.

4. Remove from the pan and allow to rest at room temperature for 15 to 20 minutes before carving. Potatoes, carrots, and onions may be roasted in the pan with the lamb. Baste them occasionally. Serve with gravy and/or mint jelly. Leftovers provide a great excuse to make shepherd's pie the next day.

SERVES 8 TO 10

HERMITS

◆

1¼ cups seedless raisins

2½ cups all-purpose flour

½ teaspoon baking soda

1 teaspoon cream of tartar

½ teaspoon salt

½ teaspoon ground cloves

½ teaspoon ground cinnamon

½ teaspoon ground allspice

½ teaspoon ground ginger

½ teaspoon ground nutmeg

½ cup (1 stick) unsalted butter, softened

1 cup sugar

¼ cup milk

1. Chop the raisins fine in a food processor with ¼ cup of the flour.

2. Sift 2 cups of the flour with the baking soda, cream of tartar, salt, and spices.

3. In a separate bowl, cream the butter and sugar.

4. Add the dry ingredients alternately with the milk to the butter-sugar mixture until well blended.

5. Stir in the raisins and enough additional flour—up to ¾ cup—to make a stiff dough.

6. Shape into 2 logs, about 1½ inches in diameter. Refrigerate overnight or freeze.

7. When ready to make, preheat the oven to 375°F., slice to desired thickness, and bake until done (15 to 20 minutes).

MAKES 3 TO 4 DOZEN COOKIES

NOTE These are the best homemade "slice and serve" cookies. The dough freezes beautifully in logs that can be kept on hand for fresh cookies baked in minutes. They may be sliced thinly and baked quickly for elegant, crisp tea cookies, or sliced ¼ inch or more thick and baked in a slower oven until just set for a rich, chewy, New England hermit.

Rancho La Puerta

Tecate,
Baja California,
Mexico

A FESTIVE DINNER

•

Mexican Roasted
Corn Soup

Jicama, Red Onion, and
Orange Salad

Chilies Rellenos with
Salsa Ranchera
Colorado,
Mexican Rice, and
Black Bean Frijoles

Strawberry-Banana
Sorbet

Rancho La Puerta, southeast of San Diego, was a foray we made just over the border into Mexico. It was started in the 1940s as a health camp for those interested in the early Christian sect of Essenes. Guests like Aldous and Laura Huxley brought their own tents, ate simple and nutritious food from the garden, and took hikes on the sacred land around Mt. Cuchuma. Today guests stay in luxurious villas, have access to a full health and exercise program, and eat nutritious and innovative meals created by Chef Bill Wavrin from the now elaborate gardens, which guests are invited to visit. His aim is to provide world-class food that's healthful, and we were dazzled by the beauty and variety at every meal. Dining on the terrace, looking out to the desert and the sacred mountain beyond, was sublime.

MEXICAN ROASTED CORN SOUP

•

1 onion, chopped

1 stalk celery, chopped

1 teaspoon olive oil

2 garlic cloves

$\frac{1}{2}$ baked potato, chopped

2 tablespoons chopped fresh oregano

8 corn cobs, husked (remove the kernels from 7 ears and save 1 to be toasted; see Note)

Low-sodium soy sauce to taste

Black pepper to taste

1 quart vegetable stock

1. In a soup pot over medium heat, sauté the onion and celery in oil until golden, approximately 10 to 12 minutes.

2. Add the garlic, potato, 1 tablespoon of the oregano, the corn kernels, soy sauce, and the pepper.

3. Sauté for 10 minutes and add the stock. Simmer until the potato is soft.

4. Puree well, return to the soup pot, and simmer for 5 minutes.

5. Garnish with the toasted corn kernels and remaining tablespoon of oregano. Serve hot.

SERVES 6 TO 8

NOTE Toast the corn cob over an open flame or grill until golden brown, taking care not to burn the kernels. Remove the kernels from the cob and set aside. You can toast more ears if you care for more smoky flavor.

JÍCAMA, RED ONION, AND ORANGE SALAD

◆

2 garlic cloves, minced

1 teaspoon finely chopped fresh oregano

4 oranges, 2 peeled and segmented and 2 juiced

¼ cup balsamic vinegar

Pinch black pepper

2 heads red romaine lettuce, washed and coarsely chopped

1 medium jícama, peeled and cut into 3-inch julienne

1 red onion, sliced

4 sprigs fresh oregano, for garnish

1. To make the dressing: Place the garlic, oregano, orange juice, vinegar, and pepper in a bowl and stir. Set aside.

2. Arrange the lettuce on 4 chilled plates, and top with the jícama and onion.

3. Toss the orange segments in the dressing and divide them evenly over the four salads.

4. Serve with the dressing on the side and a sprig of oregano for garnish.

SERVES 4

CHILIES RELLENOS
◆

6 *6- to 8-inch Anaheim or poblano chilies*

1 *pound low-sodium part-skim Monterey Jack cheese, cut into small cubes*

4 *egg whites*

1 *whole egg*

1 *garlic clove, minced fine*

1 *teaspoon chopped fresh oregano*

¼ *teaspoon salt*

2 *tablespoons whole-wheat flour*

   Canola or olive oil

   Salsa Ranchero Colorado (recipe follows)

   Mexican Rice (see page 91)

   Black Bean Frijoles (see page 92)

   Seasonal vegetables, as desired

1. Wash the chilies and toast them over an open flame until the skins are lightly charred all over. Place in a paper or plastic bag and let rest for 10 to 12 minutes. Carefully remove as much skin as possible. With a knife, make a lengthwise slit about 2 inches long just below the stem of each chili and carefully remove all the seeds from inside. Carefully insert one cheese cube into the slit in each chili.

2. Preheat the oven to 375°F.

3. Beat the egg whites until doubled in volume, then beat in the whole egg, garlic, oregano, and salt. Continue to beat until the mixture is again doubled in volume or has achieved a soft peak.

4. Sprinkle the flour on a plate or cookie sheet and dredge the chilies in the flour to coat all sides.

5. Lightly spray a sauté pan with some canola oil and place over medium-high heat. Dip each chili into the egg batter and gently place all of the chilies in the sauté pan, toasting approximately 5 minutes on each side. Place the chilies on a cookie sheet and bake for 15 to 18 minutes.

6. To serve, place each chili on a dish, and ladle a 1-ounce portion of Salsa Ranchero Colorado over the top. Accompany with 2 ounces of Mexican Rice, 2 ounces of Black Bean Frijoles, and seasonal vegetables.

SERVES 6

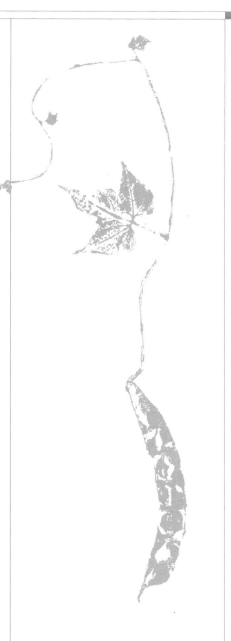

Salsa Ranchera Colorado

◆

1 onion, peeled and cut into quarters

3 tomatoes, cut into quarters

3 garlic cloves, peeled

1 medium jalapeño chili, stemmed and seeded

3 ancho chilies, lightly toasted

1 chili de arbole (dry), lightly toasted

1 tablespoon chopped fresh oregano

1 teaspoon chopped fresh cilantro

½ teaspoon salt, or to taste

1 plum tomato, cut into small dice

1 yellow jubilee tomato, cut into small dice

1. Place all of the ingredients except the tomatoes in a sauce pan with 1½ cups of water over medium heat. Bring to a simmer and cook for 30 minutes. Drain all the water and reserve.

2. Place all the mixture in a mortar, blender, or food processor and grind or blend just until chunky. You may need to use the reserved water to adjust the consistency of the salsa. Keep warm and add the plum and yellow tomatoes just before serving. Refrigerate after use. Keeps for 3 to 5 days.

MAKES ABOUT 2 CUPS

MEXICAN RICE

◆

1 onion, diced

1 stalk celery, diced

1 carrot, diced

1 teaspoon olive oil

1 medium tomato, diced

2 garlic cloves, minced

1 chili de arbole or Thai chili, toasted

1 cup brown rice

3 cups vegetable stock or water

1 tablespoon low-sodium soy sauce

1 teaspoon chopped fresh oregano

1 teaspoon chopped fresh cilantro

1. In a soup pot over medium heat, sauté the onion, celery, and carrot in oil until the onion is golden.

2. Add the tomato, garlic, chili, rice, stock, and soy sauce. Bring to a boil.

3. Reduce to a very low simmer and cook, covered, for 45 minutes.

4. Add the herbs and serve hot as a side accompaniment or cold as a rice salad with freshly blanched seasonal vegetables.

SERVES 6

NOTE You can add fresh peas when in season at the end, while the rice is hot.

Black Bean Frijoles

◆

½ *cup pinto beans, cleaned and soaked for 24 hours*

½ *cup black beans, cleaned and soaked for 24 hours*

½ *onion, peeled and chopped*

2 *garlic cloves, peeled and chopped*

3 *ancho chilies, seeded and cleaned*

1 *chili de arbole, seeded and cleaned*

1 *tablespoon chopped fresh oregano*

   Black pepper to taste

1 *quart vegetable stock or water (you will*
     have to add more as the beans cook)

   Juice of 3 limes

1 *teaspoon salt (optional)*

1. Drain the beans and place them in a stockpot.

2. Add the onion, garlic, chilies, oregano, pepper, and vegetable stock. Bring to a boil. Reduce to a simmer and cook for 2 hours, or until the beans are soft. Drain, but reserve the cooking liquid.

3. Place the beans in a food processor and puree. Use the reserved liquid to adjust the consistency. The beans should be firm and moist, like fluffy mashed potatoes.

4. Add the lime juice and salt, if desired. Mix well and serve hot.

SERVES 6 GENEROUSLY

STRAWBERRY-BANANA SORBET

◆

4 cups strawberries, hulled and washed

1 banana, peeled

1 cup orange juice

Zest and juice of 2 limes

1 kiwi, peeled and chopped

6 sprigs fresh mint, for garnish

1. Put all of the ingredients except the mint in a blender and blend until smooth. Pour into a freezerproof container measuring approximately 8 × 12 inches and freeze for at least 2 hours.

2. Transfer the mixture to a food processor and process until fluffy and smooth. Return to the freezer for at least 2 hours before serving.

3. Place 6 dessert cups in the freezer 20 minutes prior to serving. To soften the sorbet, remove from the freezer and place in the refrigerator 10 minutes prior to serving. Scoop the sorbet with an ice-cream scoop. Garnish each serving with a mint leaf and serve immediately.

SERVES 6

NOTE You may use any of your favorite fruits (except pineapple, which is high in fiber) and mango, apple, or grape juice in place of, or along with, the orange juice.

Rose Hill

Aiken,
South Carolina

FOURTH OF JULY
SOUTH
CAROLINA
BARBECUE

♦

Slow-Roasted Pig

Mustard Barbecue
Sauce

South Carolina Hash

white rice

sliced white bread

coleslaw

Chocolate Pear Tart*

*Thanks to the Chevrier Family

Located thirty minutes northeast of Augusta, Georgia, this newly restored turn-of-the-century mansion is set on four acres of camellias, azaleas, Chinese holly, and other exotic trees, shrubs, and flowers. A small and lovely chapel was added when this was an Episcopal retreat. It is now reopening as Rose Hill College, centered around Orthodox principles of thought, worship, and community life, though visitors will be welcome when there is room.

Preparation of this traditional South Carolina barbecue begins after 10:00 P.M. the night before the celebration, when the hardwood fire is lit in the barbecue pit. Guests wander through the courtyard the next day, chatting with the chef as he tends the fire and cooks the pig. The chef, Ramon Ergle, a multitalented member of the Rose Hill family, also serves as pastor of Redcliff Baptist Church, chief of the buildings at Rose Hill, and all-night theologian.

People are busy in the spacious kitchen all day, making rice, salads, and dessert. Then, as the day cools, all gather together for this bountiful feast.

SLOW-ROASTED PIG

◆

One 100-pound pig

1 recipe Mustard Barbecue Sauce (recipe follows)

1. Build a pit out of concrete blocks and a grill.

2. Start the hardwood fire about 10:00 P.M. the night before the barbecue and allow it to burn until it becomes glowing embers. You must keep this going during the entire cooking process to provide enough heat to cook the meat.

3. Grill the pig, skin side down, for 6 hours, keeping it cooking by shoveling the embers under the grate.

4. Turn the pig over and cook for about 4 hours, or until it looks as though it is falling apart. For the last couple of hours, baste with the sauce.

5. Cut the meat from the bone and pour the sauce over it.

SERVES THE NEIGHBORHOOD
(ABOUT 30 POUNDS OF MEAT)

MUSTARD BARBECUE SAUCE

◆

4 cups yellow mustard

2 cups white vinegar

3 pounds margarine

½ cup black pepper

Salt to taste

Louisiana Peto Hot Sauce to taste (optional)

Place all of the ingredients in a large kettle and cook for 1 hour over low heat.

SOUTH CAROLINA HASH

◆

21 pounds chuck roast

7 pounds Boston butt pork

2 tablespoons red pepper flakes, plus more to taste

10 pounds onions, chopped

5 pounds butter

11½ cups vinegar

2 tablespoons white pepper

Black pepper

1. Cover the chuck roast, butt pork, 2 tablespoons of red pepper flakes, and half the onions with water and cook slowly until the meat falls apart.

2. Cool. Pull the meat into strings with your hands and then return it to the broth.

3. Add the remaining 5 pounds of onions. Cook over low heat, stirring. Add the butter, vinegar, white pepper, red pepper flakes to taste, and black pepper. Continue cooking until well combined and very hot. Serve over white rice.

SERVES THE NEIGHBORHOOD

CHOCOLATE PEAR TART

♦

3 eggs

Pinch salt

1½ cups all-purpose flour

1 cup sugar

½ (1 stick) cup butter, cut into small pieces

3 ounces dark baking chocolate

1 cup sour cream, plus 2 tablespoons for chocolate sauce

2 16-ounce cans pear halves in syrup or 2 pounds
poached fresh pears

3 eggs

¾ cup milk

1. Preheat the oven to 350°F.

2. Beat 1 egg with the salt, flour, ½ cup of sugar, and butter. Chill for 1 hour.

3. Roll out and place in a greased 8-inch pie pan.

4. Melt the chocolate very slowly with 1 cup of sour cream and ½ cup of sugar until it tastes sweet. Pour over the pastry.

5. Cut the pears into thin slices and place over the chocolate filling.

6. Beat the remaining 2 eggs, 2 tablespoons of sour cream, and the milk, and pour over the pears.

7. Bake for 35 to 40 minutes. Serve a little warm.

SERVES 6

ANNUAL CLERGY CONFERENCE BRUNCH

❖

Low-Country She-
Crab Soup with Sherry

Crab, Spinach, Swiss,
and Onion Quiche

Charleston Shrimp and
Grits with Bacon
Strips and Sliced
Tomatoes

Buttermilk Biscuits

Saint Christopher
Mud Pie

Huguenot Torte

Some years ago we spent a winter in Charleston, South Carolina, and were often guests at the Carolina Yacht Club for their fabulous Southern buffets. What a pleasure to discover that Chef Stephen Boyle is now nearby at this Episcopal center and that his skills at the buffet table are still intact. This lovely retreat sits on the edge of the water, with miles of beachfront to explore, and deer, bobcats, pelicans, and bottlenose dolphins in abundance. The nearby rustic seaside chapel draws guests for quiet moments.

LOW-COUNTRY SHE-CRAB SOUP WITH SHERRY

❖

3 tablespoons unsalted butter or margarine

6 tablespoons unbleached white flour

½ teaspoon salt

1 teaspoon dried tarragon

1 tablespoon Old Bay Seasoning

½ teaspoon white pepper

1 teaspoon dried dill

1 teaspoon dried rosemary

⅛ teaspoon ground mace

¼ cup sugar

2 chicken bouillon cubes, dissolved in a little hot water

1 quart milk

½ cup heavy cream

2 cups white crabmeat or claw meat

⅓ cup she-crab roe

Sherry, warmed

1. Melt the butter in a double boiler and blend with the flour. Cook for 10 minutes.

2. Add the salt, spices and herbs, and sugar. Add the dissolved bouillon cubes and stir well. Add the milk and cream (unwhipped).

3. Cook slowly until the mixture thickens, then add the crabmeat and roe. Add the warmed sherry to individual servings, according to taste.

SERVES 6

CRAB, SPINACH, SWISS, AND ONION QUICHE

◆

PASTRY

1½ cups unbleached white flour

¼ cup (½ stick) unsalted butter

4 egg yolks

¼ cup grated Parmesan cheese

Pinch each salt, cayenne, and dry mustard

1 to 3 tablespoons ice-cold milk

1 egg white

CUSTARD

1 cup heavy cream

4 egg yolks

Pinch each salt, cayenne, and ground nutmeg

FILLING

2 pounds fresh spinach

¼ pound fresh crabmeat

¼ cup melted butter

Salt and pepper to taste

1 cup grated Gruyère cheese

1. Preheat the oven to 450°F.

To make the pastry:

2. Place the flour in a bowl. Make a well in the center of the flour. Put the butter, egg yolks, cheese, salt, cayenne, and dry mustard into the well. With the fingers of one hand, work all the center ingredients into a smooth paste. Quickly work in the flour. Add only enough ice-cold milk, 1 tablespoon at a time, to make the dough gather.

3. Shape the dough into a smooth ball. Roll it out on a floured surface. Line an ungreased 8 × 10-inch deep-dish pie plate or a quiche pan, being careful not to stretch the pastry. Prick all over the inner surfaces, including the sides, with the tines of a fork. Paint the surface with a very small amount of unbeaten egg white.

4. Partially bake the shell on the lowest oven rack for 8 to 12 minutes, or until it is lightly browned and set. Check the shell after 5 minutes and gently push down the puffy spots. Repeat if necessary. Cool the partially baked crust for about 10 minutes. Reduce the oven temperature to 375°F.

To make the custard:

5. Blend all the ingredients together.

To make the filling:

6. Wash the spinach several times. Cook in a large pot over a high heat, using only the water that clings to the leaves after the final washing. As soon as the spinach is completely wilted, remove from the heat. Drain thoroughly. Squeeze small handfuls as hard as possible to eliminate all the moisture and place in a bowl. Add the crabmeat, melted butter, and salt and pepper. Stir in the cheese.

7. Fill the prepared quiche shell with the filling. Pour the custard over the filling.

8. Bake at 375°F. for 40 to 45 minutes, or until the custard is set and the pastry is brown. Allow to rest for 3 to 4 minutes before serving.

SERVES 6

Charleston Shrimp and Grits with Bacon Strips and Sliced Tomatoes

◆

2 tablespoons chopped onion

3 tablespoons bacon grease or butter

1½ cups small raw shrimp, peeled

1 cup water

1½ tablespoons unsalted butter

1½ tablespoons unbleached white flour

1 cup milk

Salt and pepper to taste

1 teaspoon Worcestershire sauce

Grits, bacon strips, and sliced tomatoes

1. Sauté the onion in the bacon grease. When the onion is translucent, add the shrimp. Then add 1 cup of water and simmer for 2 to 3 minutes.

2. In a separate pan, melt the butter and gradually add the flour. Mix well while still over the flame and add the milk, salt and pepper, and Worcestershire.

3. Add this *roux* to the shrimp mixture and allow it to thicken.

4. Serve with hot grits and garnish with bacon strips and sliced tomatoes.

SERVES 4 TO 6

Buttermilk Biscuits

◆

2 cups unbleached white flour

¾ teaspoon salt

2 teaspoons baking powder

½ teaspoon baking soda

3 heaping tablespoons vegetable shortening

1 cup buttermilk

1. Preheat the oven to 450°F.

2. Sift the dry ingredients together, and cut in the shortening. Make a well in the center of the flour mixture. Pour in the buttermilk, and mix lightly with a fork. Place on a floured cloth, and knead for about 1 minute.

3. Roll the dough out to about ½ inch thickness and cut it into biscuits using a small cutter. Place the biscuits ½ inch apart on an ungreased cookie sheet. Bake for about 10 minutes, until golden.

MAKES 2 DOZEN BISCUITS

Saint Christopher Mud Pie

◆

1 quart chocolate ice cream, softened

1 store-bought Oreo pie shell (freeze before using)

1 8-ounce container Mellocream fudge topping

1. Spoon the ice cream into the shell and smooth the surface with a spatula. Place the pie in the freezer for at least 2 hours, or until the ice cream is very hard.

2. Spoon the fudge topping over the ice cream and spread, using a metal knife or spatula. Return to the freezer for 1 hour, or until the fudge hardens.

SERVES 6

HUGUENOT TORTE

◆

4 eggs

3 cups sugar

½ cup unbleached white flour

5 teaspoons baking powder

½ teaspoon salt

2 cups peeled and chopped Granny Smith apples

2 cups chopped pecans or walnuts

2 teaspoons vanilla extract

Whipped cream

1. Preheat the oven to 325°F.

2. Beat the eggs with a mixer until very frothy and lemon-colored.

3. Add the remaining ingredients, except the whipped cream, in the order above and pour into two 8 × 8-inch greased baking pans.

4. Bake for 30 to 45 minutes, or until brown and crisp. Serve with whipped cream.

SERVES 6 TO 8

Saint Francis
Friends of the Poor

New York, New York

St. Francis Friends of the Poor is a retreat of a different kind. The three St. Francis residences offer permanent housing with supportive services to almost three hundred men and women with long histories of chronic mental illness. They seek to offer safe, decent, humane, affordable housing to this fragile, once homeless, population. They do this with grace and joy. And with delicious, healthful food. Father John Felice, O.F.M., one of the founders, shares these family recipes.

AN ITALIAN BUFFET

◆

Escarole Soup with Meatballs

Penne al Pomodoro e Basilico

Bruschetta

Chicken and Potatoes

Spinach and Beans

Fresh Fruit and cheese

ESCAROLE SOUP WITH MEATBALLS

◆

1 2½- to 3-pound chicken

2 medium carrots, peeled and sliced

2 celery stalks, sliced

1 medium yellow onion, chopped

2 bay leaves

2 quarts cold water, or enough to cover the chicken well
   Salt and freshly ground black pepper to taste

1 large head escarole, chopped into 1-inch pieces

1 pound lean chopped meat

½ cup bread crumbs

1 egg, beaten

¼ cup grated Parmesan cheese

1 garlic clove, minced

¼ cup chopped fresh Italian parsley

1. Put the chicken, carrots, celery, onion, bay leaves, water, and salt and pepper to taste into a large soup pot. Bring to a boil. Skim off any foam that may surface. Simmer for 2 hours.

2. Remove the chicken, debone it, cut up the meat, and return the meat to the soup.

3. Boil the escarole in a separate pot of water for 30 seconds to remove the bitterness. Drain and add to the soup.

4. In a large bowl, mix the chopped meat, bread crumbs, egg, Parmesan, garlic, parsley, and salt and pepper to taste.

5. Using the palms of your hands, roll into meatballs 1 inch in diameter.

6. When you are ready to serve the soup, bring it back to a boil and drop in the meatballs. When they float to the surface (about 3 minutes), the soup is ready.

SERVES 4, WITH DELICIOUS LEFTOVERS
FOR LUNCH THE NEXT DAY

PENNE AL POMODORO E BASILICO

◆

2 tablespoons extra-virgin olive oil

1 medium yellow onion, chopped

1 28-ounce can imported Italian plum tomatoes

Salt

Freshly ground white pepper

1 pound penne (or any pasta of choice)

10 to 12 leaves fresh basil, chopped

Freshly grated Parmesan cheese

1. Heat the olive oil and sauté the onion for about 5 minutes, or until golden.

2. Add the tomatoes (reserve the juice to use if the sauce is too thick) and salt and pepper to taste. Break down the tomatoes with a spoon as they cook. Simmer for 20 to 25 minutes.

3. Cook the penne, toss with the sauce, and top with the chopped fresh basil.

4. Serve hot, with plenty of freshly grated Parmesan cheese.

SERVES 4

BRUSCHETTA

◆

This is best prepared on an outdoor grill, but an oven broiler will suffice.

6 plum tomatoes, seeded and chopped

1 small red onion, chopped fine

1 tablespoon extra-virgin olive oil, plus additional for
      brushing on bread

   Pinch oregano

   Salt and freshly ground black pepper to taste

8 to 10 fresh basil leaves

8 slices Italian bread

1. Mix the tomatoes, onion, 1 tablespoon of oil, oregano, salt, and pepper and marinate for at least 30 minutes. Just before serving, chop the basil leaves and add to the mixture.

2. Brush one side of each slice of bread with olive oil. Grill both sides of the bread until lightly toasted.

3. Place the tomato mixture on top of the side of the grilled bread that has oil on it. Serve warm.

SERVES 4

CHICKEN AND POTATOES

◆

1 large yellow onion, peeled, halved, and sliced

1 2½- to 3-pound chicken, cut into 8 pieces

2 large potatoes, peeled and cut lengthwise into
      8 wedges each

   Salt, pepper, and dried oregano to taste

   Extra-virgin olive oil

1. Preheat the oven to 375°F.

2. In a baking pan, scatter the sliced onion. Place the chicken pieces, skin down, over the onion. Place the potato wedges around the chicken. Add salt and a generous amount of freshly ground black pepper. Liberally sprinkle dried oregano over the chicken and potatoes. Drizzle olive oil over the dish. Cover with tin foil and bake for 45 minutes.

3. Remove from the oven. Turn the chicken pieces over so that they are skin-side up. Place back in the oven, uncovered, for 45 minutes, or until the chicken is golden-brown and cooked through.

SERVES 4

SPINACH AND BEANS
◆

2 tablespoons extra-virgin olive oil

2 garlic cloves, sliced thin

2 packages (10 ounces each) frozen spinach or 1 pound washed fresh spinach

1 16-ounce can cannellini beans

Salt and freshly ground black pepper to taste

1. Heat the olive oil in a large pot and sauté the garlic for 1 minute.

2. Add the spinach and cook for 5 minutes.

3. Heat the cannellini beans in their juice. Add these to the spinach, stir, and cook until hot, adding a little water if necessary. At the last minute, add salt and pepper.

SERVES 4

For a description of the center, see page 15 in the breakfast section.

CREAM CHEESE LASAGNA

◆

1 pound ground turkey

¾ cup chopped onion

1 8-ounce can tomato sauce

1 6-ounce can tomato paste

¼ cup water

1 tablespoon dried parsley

½ teaspoon dried oregano

½ teaspoon fennel seeds

½ teaspoon dried basil

2 bay leaves

1 teaspoon beef-flavored bouillon granules (optional)

1 garlic clove, minced

8 ounces cream cheese, softened

1 cup cottage cheese

½ cup chopped scallion

¼ cup sour cream

2 eggs, beaten

8 ounces lasagna noodles, cooked and drained

2 cups shredded mozzarella cheese

½ cup grated Parmesan cheese

½ cup shredded Cheddar

Green pepper rings

Saint Mary's
Episcopal Retreat and
Conference Center

Sewanee,
Tennessee

BOARD LUNCHEON

◆

Cream Cheese Lasagna

Homemade Rolls

Tossed Salad with
Poppy Seed Dressing

Quick Peanut-Butter
Fudge

1. Preheat the oven to 350°F.

2. Cook the turkey and onion in a heavy skillet until browned, stirring to crumble the turkey; drain. Stir in the tomato sauce, tomato paste, water, parsley, oregano, fennel seeds, basil, bay leaves, bouillon granules, and garlic; cook over low heat for 10 minutes; discard the bay leaves.

3. Combine the cream cheese, cottage cheese, scallion, sour cream, and eggs; stir well.

4. Spoon a small amount of the turkey sauce into a lightly greased 12 × 8 × 2-inch baking dish. Layer the lasagna noodles, cheese mixture, and mozzarella and Parmesan cheeses over the turkey, then repeat all the layers, including the turkey. Sprinkle with Cheddar cheese.

5. Cover and bake for 30 minutes. Top the lasagna with green pepper rings. Let stand 10 minutes before serving.

SERVES 6 TO 8

HOMEMADE ROLLS
◆

1 package dry yeast

3 tablespoons sugar

¼ cup warm water

2½ cups unbleached white flour

½ cup vegetable shortening

1 cup buttermilk

1. Mix the yeast and sugar. Stir in the water. Add the flour, then mix the shortening in with a fork until the consistency is like coarse meal. Add the buttermilk; cover. Let stand in a warm place until doubled in size.

2. Preheat the oven to 425°F.

3. Turn the dough out onto a floured board. Knead, roll, and cut it into 2 dozen rolls. Fold the rolls over and put them onto a greased baking sheet. Allow them to rise once more and then bake until brown, about 10 to 12 minutes.

MAKES ABOUT 2 DOZEN ROLLS

POPPY SEED DRESSING
◆

1½ cups olive oil

⅔ cup honey

½ cup balsamic vinegar

4 tablespoons poppy seeds

2 tablespoons minced onion or shallot

2 tablespoons Dijon mustard

1 teaspoon salt

1. Combine all of the ingredients in a blender. Process on low speed for 30 seconds.

2. Cover and chill. Stir well before serving.

MAKES ALMOST 3 CUPS

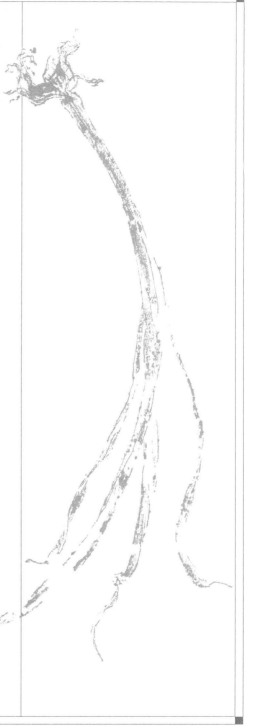

QUICK PEANUT-BUTTER FUDGE

◆

$\frac{1}{3}$ cup margarine

$\frac{1}{2}$ cup light corn syrup

$\frac{3}{4}$ cup peanut butter

$\frac{1}{2}$ teaspoon salt

1 teaspoon vanilla extract

$4\frac{1}{2}$ cups confectioners' sugar, sifted

$\frac{3}{4}$ cup chopped nuts

1. Combine the margarine, corn syrup, peanut butter, salt, and vanilla in a large bowl. Stir in the sugar gradually.

2. Turn onto a board and knead until well blended and smooth.

3. Add the nuts, kneading them into the fudge.

4. Press out with your hands or a rolling pin until $\frac{1}{2}$ inch thick and cut into pieces $1\frac{1}{2}$ inches square.

SERVES 4 TO 6

After the long, harrowing drive to this center high in remote mountainous northwest North Carolina, even spartan fare seemed like a feast. With the welcoming and gracious staff joining us around the dinner table, and the fire roaring in the adjoining library fireplace, we felt serene. The center is unusual in that it was founded to welcome a variety of Buddhist teachers and traditions. It now hosts twenty-one such retreats a year in a beautiful, handcrafted meditation hall that's always open. Much of the fine woodwork in the main lodge was done by a craftsman so devoted to the task that he continued to make the daily trip, even after a crippling accident, until the work was complete. This simple, hearty, healthful fare is just right for a time of retreat and as sustenance before a hike up into the glorious mountains.

Southern Dharma Retreat Center

Hot Springs, North Carolina

SIMPLY HEALTHFUL

◆

Oh You Beautiful Dal

Spelt Bread

Green Salad with Tahini-Basil Dressing

Favorite Brownies*

*Thanks to Nestlé.

OH YOU BEAUTIFUL DAL

◆

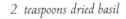

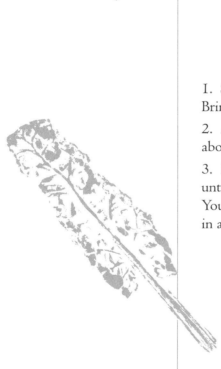

2 *teaspoons dried basil*

1 *teaspoon black pepper*

3 *teaspoons ground cumin*

1 *teaspoon grated fresh ginger*

3 *tablespoons oil*

9 *cups water*

3 *teaspoons salt*

2 *cups spinach, collard greens, or chard*

3 *cups split peas*

2 *teaspoons honey*

2 *tablespoons lemon juice*

Tamari (optional)

1. Sauté the spices in oil. Add the water, salt, and greens. Bring to a boil.

2. Add the split peas and simmer, stirring frequently, for about an hour.

3. Lower the heat and cook, stirring even more frequently, until soft. Add the honey and lemon juice. Adjust the flavor. You may wish to add tamari. Serve immediately or keep hot in a double boiler.

SERVES 12

SPELT BREAD

◆

2 packages yeast

2½ cups lukewarm water

½ cup honey

2 tablespoons oil

2 teaspoons salt

6 cups spelt flour (obtainable in health food stores)

1. Dissolve the yeast in the water and let sit until active. Mix all the wet ingredients into the dry. Knead for 5 to 7 minutes. Shape the loaves into oiled pans. Let them rise for 30 minutes in a 100°F. oven, or until doubled.

2. Remove the pans from the oven and increase the temperature to 350°F.

3. Bake for 30 to 45 minutes.

MAKES 2 LOAVES

TAHINI-BASIL DRESSING

◆

½ cup tahini

½ cup water

¼ cup lemon juice

3 tablespoons tamari

Dash hot sauce

Handful chopped fresh basil

Whip all the ingredients together.

MAKES 2 CUPS

FAVORITE BROWNIES

◆

2 cups Nestlé semisweet chocolate chips

½ cup (1 stick) unsalted butter, cut into pieces

3 eggs, beaten

1¼ cups unbleached all-purpose flour

1 cup sugar

¼ teaspoon baking soda

1 teaspoon vanilla extract

½ cup chopped walnuts

1. Preheat the oven to 350°F.

2. Melt 1 cup of the chips and the butter in a large, heavy saucepan over a low heat and stir until smooth. Remove from the heat.

3. Add the eggs and stir well.

4. Add the flour, sugar, baking soda, and vanilla; stir well.

5. Stir in the remaining cup of chocolate chips and the nuts.

6. Spread into a greased 9 × 13-inch baking pan. Bake for 18 to 22 minutes, or until a toothpick inserted in the center comes out slightly sticky. Let cool and cut into 2-inch squares.

MAKES 2 DOZEN BROWNIES

This Benedictine monastery, near Binghamton, is on the route we often take to our hometown in upstate New York, and we always stop there. The nuns are warm and welcoming, their Susquehanna Valley views beautiful, and their food divine. Sister Mary Placid's mother was a chef in southern France and passed on her skills and recipes to her daughter, who is working on her own cookbook, to be called *Wind of the Spirit.* Supper here is brought to the guest house in a basket by Sister Jeanne Marie, with platters and bowls of wonderful French country cooking appearing each evening. The main meal is often taken in silence with the community, following noon prayer in the simple chapel. With windows looking out to the mountains, the dining room is filled with roasted meats, poultry, vegetables, and some wine from their own winery, bottled under the St. Benedict Winery label. Desserts often include the monastery's luscious raspberries, which are also used in one of their wines—truly heavenly feasts!

Transfiguration Monastery

Windsor, New York

HOLIDAY FEAST

•

Basque Shrimp and Mushrooms in White Wine

Roast Chicken

Vegetables from Bordeaux-Basque Cuisine

Strawberry Compote

BASQUE SHRIMP AND MUSHROOMS IN WHITE WINE

◆

2 cups canned or homemade chicken broth

2 cups dry white wine (French or Italian)

3 teaspoons olive oil

1 cup sliced mushrooms

½ cup minced onion

⅓ cup finely chopped red and yellow bell pepper

1 teaspoon grated lemon peel or juice

2 teaspoons chopped fresh parsley

2 teaspoons chopped fresh celery

½ cup olives (black or green)

Pinch each salt and pepper

1 pound large or medium raw shrimp, peeled and cleaned

2 teaspoons dried oregano or Sister Placid's "Special Spices" (see Note)

1. Place the chicken broth and wine in a saucepan. Boil gently until reduced by half.

2. Add the oil, mushrooms, onion, pepper, lemon, parsley, celery, olives, salt, and pepper and cook, stirring constantly with a wooden spoon or fork.

3. After about 15 minutes, add the shrimp and oregano and cook for another 5 to 7 minutes, until the shrimp are opaque.

SERVES 6 TO 8

NOTE "Special Spices" are available from the Transfiguration Monastery for $3.50 (see Names and Addresses in the back).

ROAST CHICKEN

◆

   2 *whole chickens, cut up*

      White flour

$\frac{1}{2}$ *cup olive oil*

  1 *cup water*

$\frac{1}{2}$ *tablespoon honey*

$\frac{1}{2}$ *cup vinegar (strawberry if available)*

  2 *teaspoons cornstarch*

1. Preheat the oven to 375°F.

2. Roll the chicken pieces in a little flour. Heat the oil in a pan, add the chicken, and brown well.

3. Combine the water, honey, vinegar, and cornstarch.

4. Place the chicken in an ovenproof dish and add the sauce. Cook for $\frac{1}{2}$ hour.

SERVES 6 TO 8

Vegetables from Bordeaux-Basque Cuisine

◆

10 large potatoes

2 tablespoons olive oil

1 cup chopped onion

½ cup chopped fresh parsley

1 teaspoon dried mixed herbs (see Note)

1 cup grated mozzarella cheese

1 cup sour cream

3 eggs, beaten

1 cup yellow raisins

3 teaspoons cornstarch

Pinch each salt and pepper

1. Boil the potatoes until soft and cut them into small pieces.

2. Preheat the oven to 350° F.

3. Heat the oil in a sauté pan and lightly cook the onion.

4. In a large bowl, combine the potato, onion, herbs, cheese, sour cream, eggs, raisins, cornstarch, salt, and pepper. Pour into a glass oven dish and cook for 20 minutes, or until golden-brown.

SERVES 8

NOTE Sister Placid recommends her "Fifteen Spices" herbs, available from the Transfiguration Monastery (see Names and Addresses in the back).

STRAWBERRY COMPOTE

◆

This compote can be served with cake, cookies, ice cream, or whipped cream.

> *2 cups water*
>
> *2 cups sugar*
>
> *2 pints fresh strawberries, hulled, washed, and halved*

1. Cook the water and sugar for about 5 minutes, or until syrupy.
2. Add the strawberries and bring to a boil.
3. Cook for about 5 minutes. Refrigerate.

SERVES 6 TO 8

SUNDAY SUPPER

◆

Vegetable Soup

Banana or Raisin
Omelette

Salade Niçoise

VEGETABLE SOUP

◆

2 large carrots

1 medium onion

2 stalks celery

3 medium potatoes

3 cabbage leaves (optional)

1 quart water

1 teaspoon salt

1 teaspoon Sister Placid's "Fifteen Spices"
    (see Note, page 120) or a mixture of dried
    thyme, oregano, and Italian seasoning

1 tablespoon butter

1. Chop the carrots, onion, celery, potatoes, and cabbage. Place them in a soup kettle, add the water, salt, and herbs, and bring to a boil.

2. Cook for about 25 minutes. Add the butter, stir, and serve.

SERVES 6

BANANA OR RAISIN OMELETTE

◆

4 eggs

1/4 cup milk

2 pinches salt

1 tablespoon cornstarch

3 tablespoons oil

1/2 cup raisins or 1 banana, sliced

1 tablespoon honey

1. Blend the eggs, milk, salt, and cornstarch.

2. Heat the oil in a frying pan.

3. Pour in the mixture and stir slightly. When the eggs are somewhat cooked, add the raisins or the banana, and then the honey. Be careful not to overcook.

4. Loosen the edges all around with a knife. With a spatula, turn one half over on the other and then—*pouff!*, says Sister Placid—onto the plate!

SERVES 2

SALADE NIÇOISE

◆

Lettuce (green-leaf, curly, or whatever is your favorite)
½ *small onion*
1 *scallion, including the green stalk*
2 *tablespoons olive oil*
3 *tablespoons vinegar*
Garlic croutons
Cheese

1. Fill a salad bowl with sufficient lettuce.

2. Mince the onion and scallion and sprinkle on the lettuce.

3. Mix the oil and vinegar.

4. Add to the bowl and toss the salad just before serving.

5. Sprinkle the top with garlic croutons and bits of cheese.

SERVES 6

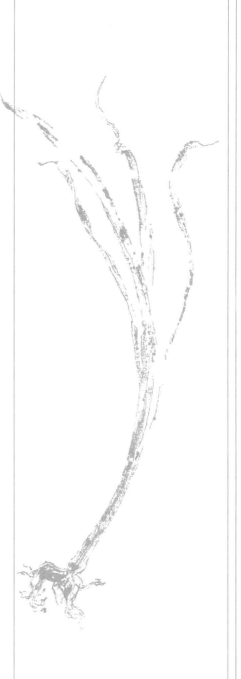

Villa Maria Del Mar

Santa Cruz,
California

SUNSET FEAST
BY THE SEA

◆

Lemon Chicken
with Thyme

Vegetable Polenta

Napa Cabbage Salad

Cheesecake with
Fresh Raspberries

We remember Villa Maria Del Mar and its Sisters of the Holy Names with great thanks and fondness. After many months on the road, we arrived at this seaside retreat south of San Francisco, in need of a retreat ourselves, since Jack had just been stricken with a painful toothache. The staff immediately took us under their collective wing, transporting Jack to a dentist who worked miracles, then settling him into a luxurious chair in front of the window, looking out at the Pacific. They plied him with soft and comforting foods, and by the next day he was able to join me in the bright seaside dining room to sample their delicious fare. Truly a home away from home for us and for the groups and individuals who are welcomed as members of the family.

LEMON CHICKEN WITH THYME

◆

3 tablespoons unbleached white flour

$\frac{1}{2}$ teaspoon salt

$\frac{1}{4}$ teaspoon pepper

4 skinless, boneless chicken breast halves

2 tablespoons olive oil

1 medium onion

1 tablespoon unsalted butter

1 cup chicken broth

3 tablespoons lemon juice

$\frac{1}{2}$ teaspoon dried thyme

Lemon wedges (optional)

2 tablespoons chopped fresh parsley (optional)

1. In a plastic or paper bag, combine the flour, salt, and pepper and shake to mix. Add the chicken and shake to coat lightly. Remove the chicken and reserve the excess seasoned flour.

2. In a large skillet, warm 1 tablespoon of oil over medium heat. Add the chicken and brown on one side for about 5 minutes. Add the remaining tablespoon of oil, turn the chicken, and brown well on the second side for about 5 minutes. Transfer the chicken to a plate and set aside.

3. Coarsely chop the onion. Add the butter to the skillet. When it melts, add the onion and cook, stirring, until softened, 2 to 3 minutes.

4. Stir in the reserved seasoned flour and cook, stirring, until the flour is completely absorbed, about 1 minute.

5. Add the broth, 2 tablespoons of the lemon juice, and the thyme and bring the mixture to a boil, stirring constantly.

6. Return the chicken to the skillet, reduce the heat to medium-low, and cover the skillet. Cook until the chicken is tender, about 5 minutes.

7. Divide the chicken among 4 plates. Stir the remaining tablespoon of lemon juice into the sauce in the skillet and pour over the chicken. Serve the chicken with lemon wedges and a sprinkling of parsley, if desired.

SERVES 4

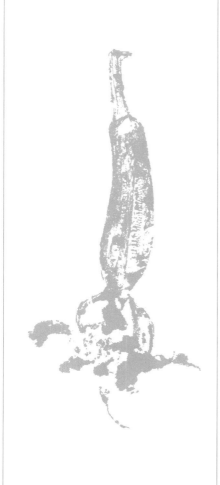

Vegetable Polenta

◆

1¼ cups polenta

3½ cups warm water

Salt and pepper to taste

Olive oil

1 small eggplant, peeled and sliced thin

1 medium zucchini, sliced

1 red bell pepper, cut into chunks

1 small onion, cut into chunks

2 8-ounce cans tomato sauce

1 14½-ounce can tomatoes, chopped

½ cup grated carrot

½ cup grated zucchini

½ cup sliced mushrooms

¼ cup chopped onion

¼ cup chopped green bell pepper

2 garlic cloves, minced

½ teaspoon dried oregano

1 bay leaf

½ teaspoon dried basil

Sprig fresh rosemary

Parmesan cheese

1. Preheat the oven to 350°F.

2. Place the polenta in a casserole. Pour warm water over the polenta and sprinkle with salt. Whisk together.

3. Place in the oven and bake for about 50 minutes, or until all the water is absorbed.

4. Heat some olive oil in a skillet. Sauté the eggplant, zucchini, red bell pepper, and onion and set aside.

5. Place the tomato sauce, tomatoes, carrot, zucchini, mushrooms, onion, green bell pepper, garlic, oregano, bay leaf, basil, rosemary, salt, and pepper in a saucepan and cook. The longer you cook this sauce the better. Add water if the sauce thickens too much.

6. Place the sautéed vegetables on top of the cooked polenta. Pour the sauce over everything and sprinkle with Parmesan cheese. Return to a 350°F. oven and cook until bubbly.

SERVES 4 TO 6

NAPA CABBAGE SALAD

◆

2 tablespoons sugar

½ cup oil

1 teaspoon seasoned salt

½ teaspoon pepper

3 tablespoons tarragon vinegar

2 to 3 tablespoons butter

½ cup almonds

1 package Ramen noodles

1 teaspoon sesame seeds

¼ cup sesame sticks

1 head Napa cabbage, chopped

2 scallions, chopped

1. Mix the sugar, oil, salt, pepper, and vinegar thoroughly.

2. Heat the butter and sauté the almonds, noodles, sesame seeds, and sticks. Let these dry on a paper towel.

3. Add the cabbage and scallions.

4. Mix everything together and toss.

SERVES 6

CHEESECAKE WITH FRESH RASPBERRIES

◆

6 ounces cream cheese, softened

½ cup plus 1 teaspoon sugar

8 ounces Cool Whip

1 9-inch graham-cracker crust

½ pint fresh red raspberries

½ teaspoon balsamic vinegar

1. Whip together the cream cheese and ½ cup of the sugar.

2. Fold the Cool Whip into the cheese mixture.

3. Place in the pie crust.

4. Toss the raspberries in the remaining teaspoon of sugar and the balsamic vinegar, and place over the cheese.

5. Refrigerate for at least 3 hours before serving.

SERVES 6

We arrived in Mobile on a Sunday, planning to sample a famous local restaurant before checking in at this cloistered Catholic monastery built more than a hundred years ago. The restaurant was closed and we were starving. We arrived dejectedly at the wrought-iron gates of Visitation, glimpsing nuns in full habit. As we entered the reception area, the sweet smells of a Southern dinner came our way. The Sunday retreat dinner was just concluding, and the buffet had yet to be cleared. We dug into oven-baked Southern chicken and gravy, peas, tomato aspic, and dressing, and truly understood the meaning of the word gratitude! These are the recipes we include—much simpler to make than we'd expected, but truly satisfying to two weary travelers.

OVEN-BAKED SOUTHERN CHICKEN

◆

1 3-pound chicken, cut into pieces
Salt
Pepper
Garlic salt
Paprika

1. Preheat the oven to 375° F.

2. Wash the chicken, removing the skin and fat if you wish (although the meat will be more tender if you leave some of the skin and fat on).

3. Sprinkle some salt, pepper, garlic salt, and paprika in a roasting pan. Arrange the chicken in the pan and sprinkle

Visitation Monastery

Mobile,
Alabama

·

SUNDAY DINNER

◆

Oven-Baked Southern
Chicken

Rice and Gravy

Peas

Tomato Aspic and
dressing

Rolls and butter

Apple Crisp

with the same seasonings (the paprika gives a nice golden color).

4. Bake for about 45 minutes. Then place in a covered serving pan on top of the stove and steam slowly for 1 hour. Serve with rice, gravy (recipe follows), and peas.

SERVES 4 TO 6

GRAVY
◆

1 package onion-soup mix

1 can cream of chicken soup

   Drippings from chicken pan

   Worcestershire sauce or onion soup (optional)

1. Mix the onion-soup mix and cream of chicken soup.

2. Add the juice and drippings from the chicken pan. (There will be more from the steaming pan than the baking pan.) If the gravy is too thick, add Worcestershire sauce, onion soup (prepared as directed), or water to thin it out.

3. Heat in the top of a double boiler.

SERVES 4 TO 6

TOMATO ASPIC

♦

2 tablespoons unflavored gelatin

3½ cups tomato or V-8 juice

1½ cups celery tops

3 tablespoons chopped onion

1 garlic clove, chopped fine

Pinch ground cloves

1 bay leaf

¼ teaspoon freshly ground pepper

1½ teaspoons sugar

2 tablespoons lemon juice

1. In a large bowl, sprinkle the gelatin over ½ cup of the tomato juice.

2. Heat the remaining 3 cups of tomato juice with the celery tops, onion, garlic, cloves, bay leaf, pepper, and sugar. Simmer for 15 minutes.

3. Strain the hot liquid into the gelatin mixture. Add the lemon juice after the gelatin has dissolved. Pour into a mold or molds and chill until firm.

4. For a dressing, try beating some mayonnaise with half-and-half and a little lemon juice.

SERVES 8

APPLE CRISP

◆

2 pounds apples, peeled, cored, and sliced
Ground cinnamon
¾ cup quick-cooking oatmeal
½ cup unbleached white flour
¾ cup brown sugar
6 tablespoons (¾ stick) unsalted butter

1. Preheat the oven to 350°F.

2. Spread the apples in a 9 × 12-inch baking pan. Sprinkle with cinnamon.

3. In a large bowl, mix the oatmeal, flour, and sugar until well blended.

4. Melt the butter and mix with the dry ingredients until crumbly.

5. Spread over the apples.

6. Bake for about 45 minutes, or until bubbly.

SERVES 6

Chef Gernard Gowdy began his career at this 1930s Spanish-style lodge south of Tallahassee in 1949. He has recently returned to share his culinary gifts with fortunate guests at this nature preserve and conference center. From almost any table in the dining room one can watch an infinite variety of bird and water life. At dinner one evening we saw alligators floating in the spring, fish leaping by the hundreds, and birds fishing and flying everywhere. The gracious dining room is alive with activity too, with delicious local specialties at very reasonable prices. Chef Gowdy was kind enough to share some of his signature dishes with us here. Following the feasts, we recommend wandering the grounds and trails, among the live oaks, pines, and magnolias.

Wakulla Springs Lodge

Wakulla Springs,
Florida

WAKULLA SPRINGS LODGE BUFFET

◆

Navy Bean Soup

Crab Imperial

Wakulla Shrimp Supreme

Whole Baked Tomatoes with hush puppies

Fluffy Lime Cream Pie

Blueberry-Sour Cream Pie

NAVY BEAN SOUP

◆

1 pound dried navy beans

5 cups water

1 can beef consommé

1 chicken bouillon cube

4 potatoes, diced

2 onions, diced

4 tablespoons (½ stick) unsalted butter

4 carrots, diced

2 cups chopped ham

3 bay leaves

Salt and pepper to taste

1. Place the navy beans, water, consommé, and bouillon cube in a large pot. Bring to a boil and simmer for 2 hours; add the potatoes.

2. Sauté the onion in butter until partially cooked. Add to the soup pot, together with the carrots, ham, bay leaves, salt, and pepper.

3. Simmer for 1 hour, or until the vegetables are soft.

SERVES 6

CRAB IMPERIAL
◆

1 pound fresh crabmeat

¼ teaspoon salt

2 dashes Worcestershire sauce

½ teaspoon minced fresh garlic

2 stalks celery, minced

⅓ cup mayonnaise

1 teaspoon fresh lemon juice

Cracker crumbs

Parmesan cheese

Butter

1. In a bowl combine the crabmeat, salt, Worcestershire sauce, garlic, celery, mayonnaise, and lemon juice. Mix well and allow to sit for 1 hour.

2. Preheat the oven to 350°F.

3. Place the mixture in a buttered casserole dish. Top with the cracker crumbs and Parmesan cheese. Dot with butter. Bake for 20 minutes.

SERVES 4

WAKULLA SHRIMP SUPREME

◆

*1 pound (21 to 25) medium shrimp,
shelled and deveined*

*8 strips bacon, cut into 3 pieces each
(1 slice bacon per 3 shrimp)*

Toothpicks

Paprika

Butter

1. Preheat the broiler.

2. Wrap each shrimp in bacon and fasten with a toothpick. Sprinkle lightly with paprika and dot with a little butter.

3. Broil in a pan with a small amount of water to prevent sticking. Turn once when the bacon begins to crisp.

4. When cooked on both sides (about 5 minutes), remove the toothpicks and serve with hush puppies and whole baked tomatoes (recipe follows).

SERVES 4

WHOLE BAKED TOMATOES

◆

1 tomato per serving

Bread crumbs

Salt and pepper to taste

Parmesan cheese

Butter

1. Preheat the oven to 350°F.

2. Cut about a third of the pulp from the center of each tomato and fill with bread crumbs and salt and pepper to taste. Sprinkle with Parmesan cheese and dot with butter.

3. Place in a pan with a little water to prevent sticking.

4. Bake for 15 to 20 minutes. Serve with hush puppies.

FLUFFY LIME CREAM PIE

◆

CRUMB SHELL

$1\frac{1}{2}$ *cups fine graham-cracker crumbs*

$\frac{1}{4}$ *cup sugar*

$\frac{1}{3}$ *cup unsalted butter, melted*

FILLING

3 eggs, separated, at room temperature

$\frac{1}{2}$ *cup fresh lime juice (from about 4 limes)*

1 14-ounce can sweetened condensed milk

$\frac{1}{4}$ *teaspoon salt*

1 tablespoon sugar

TOPPING

1 cup heavy cream

3 tablespoons sugar, preferably superfine

4 thick lime slices, halved

1. Preheat the oven to 350°F.

To make the crumb shell:

2. In a medium bowl, combine the crumbs, sugar, and melted butter, and toss until the crumbs are coated with butter. Place in a 9-inch pie pan and lightly press over the bottom and up the sides to make a shell of even thickness. Bake for 8 minutes, until set and lightly browned. Let cool on a rack. Reduce the oven temperature to 300°F.

To make the filling:

3. In a large mixing bowl, beat the egg yolks until light in color. Gradually beat in the lime juice and then the condensed milk.

4. Using clean beaters and bowl, beat the egg whites with the salt until soft peaks form. Gradually add the sugar and continue beating until stiff peaks form. Using a rubber spatula, quickly but gently fold one third of the beaten egg whites into the yolk mixture. Fold in the remaining egg whites. Pile into the pie shell. Bake for 15 minutes. Let cool to room temperature on a rack. Refrigerate for at least 6 hours or overnight.

To make the topping:

5. Beat the cream at high speed until soft peaks form. Gradually add the sugar and continue beating until just stiff. Spread half of the whipped cream over the pie. Using a spoon or a pastry bag with a decorative tip, make 7 rosettes or mounds of whipped cream around the edge of the pie and one in the center. Top each mound with half a lime slice. Serve chilled. If you are not serving immediately, refrigerate for up to 1 hour.

SERVES 6 TO 8

BLUEBERRY–SOUR CREAM PIE

◆

1 cup sugar

½ teaspoon salt

¼ cup all-purpose flour

2 eggs

2 cups sour cream

¾ teaspoon vanilla extract

1 9-inch graham-cracker shell, unbaked

1 can blueberry pie filling

1 cup whipped cream

1. Preheat the oven to 350°F.

2. In a mixing bowl, combine the sugar, salt, flour, eggs, sour cream, and vanilla, and mix well. Pour into the pie shell and bake for 30 minutes, or until the center is set.

3. Top the hot pie with blueberry filling. Chill for several hours. When ready to serve, top with whipped cream.

SERVES 6 TO 8

The cooks in this rustic nonsectarian retreat adjacent to the redwood forests in Mendocino County are known for their skill in using local fruits, vegetables, and herbs fresh from their own gardens. Guests are needed to help with garden care and harvesting, making them truly a part of the community. One guest said, "Most meaningful for me was a midmorning meditation in the meadow. The wind blowing through the tall grass reminded me of the breath of the spirit. The redwoods were silent onlookers; the birds provided musical background." It is in this spirit that cuisines from all cultures are served in the center's cozy dining room.

Wellspring Renewal Center

Philo,
California

TAMALE PIE

•

½ cup (1 stick) unsalted butter or oil

1 cup chopped onion

4 garlic cloves, minced

1 cup chopped bell pepper

1 teaspoon dried oregano

1 teaspoon ground cumin

4 teaspoons chili powder

Salt

1 cup chopped olives

1½ cups cooked, drained kidney beans

2 cups tomato sauce

2 cups cornmeal

4 teaspoons sugar

1 teaspoon black pepper

2 eggs, beaten

A HEARTY WEEKDAY LUNCH

•

Tamale Pie with salsa
and sour cream

Barley-Corn Salad

Applesauce Cake with
Butterscotch Icing

1 cup milk

20 ounces fresh or frozen corn

1 cup grated Cheddar cheese, plus extra for sprinkling

Salsa, for serving

Sour cream, for serving

1. Preheat the oven to 350°F.

2. Melt 4 tablespoons of the butter; sauté the onion and garlic for 5 minutes, or until the onion is translucent. Add the bell pepper, oregano, cumin, chili powder, and salt. Cook for 2 to 3 minutes, or until the pepper is soft. Add the olives, beans, and tomato sauce. Simmer for another 5 minutes. Set aside.

3. Mix the cornmeal, sugar, and black pepper.

4. Melt the remaining 4 tablespoons butter.

5. In a separate bowl, mix the eggs, milk, melted butter, corn, and Cheddar cheese.

6. Combine the mixtures. Pour into a buttered 9 × 13-inch casserole pan and top with the sautéed vegetables.

7. Bake for 20 minutes, sprinkle with additional cheese, and bake for 5 more minutes. Serve with salsa and sour cream.

SERVES 8

BARLEY-CORN SALAD

◆

1 cup barley

½ cup thinly sliced scallion

1 to 2 jalapeño peppers, minced fine

3 tablespoons vinegar

⅓ cup olive oil

2 cups cooked fresh corn

1 large tomato, chopped

2 garlic cloves, minced

½ teaspoon ground cumin

¼ cup minced fresh cilantro

1. Sprinkle the barley into a large saucepan of boiling water. Stir and simmer for ½ hour, or until tender. Pour into a colander, rinse, and drain.

2. Combine the barley with all the other ingredients, except the cilantro (which should be added just before serving), and allow the flavors to blend. Serve at room temperature.

SERVES 6 TO 8

APPLESAUCE CAKE

◆

1 cup oil

2 cups sugar

3 cups applesauce

2 cups unbleached white flour

2 cups whole-wheat pastry flour

2 tablespoons cocoa powder

4 teaspoons baking soda

2 teaspoons ground cinnamon

¼ teaspoon ground nutmeg

¼ teaspoon ground cloves

1 teaspoon salt

½ cup raisins

½ cup chopped walnuts

1. Preheat the oven to 400° F.

2. Beat together the oil and sugar. Add the applesauce.

3. Sift the dry ingredients into a separate bowl. Add to the applesauce mixture. Stir in the raisins and walnuts.

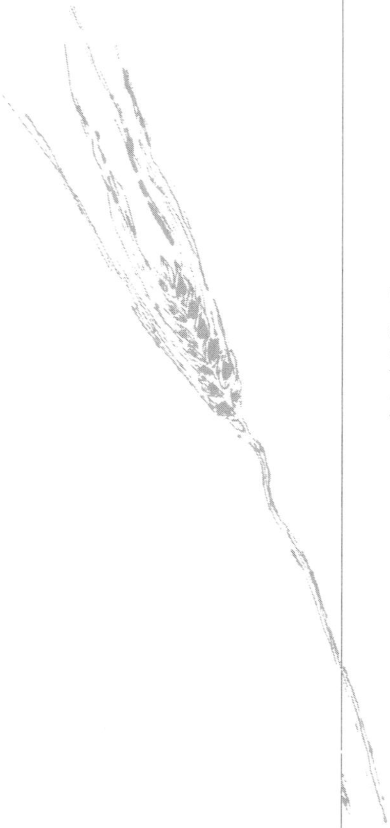

4. Bake in a 9 × 13 × 2-inch pan. After 15 minutes, turn the oven down to 350°F. for 30 minutes more, or until a toothpick inserted in the center comes out clean.

5. When cool, frost with Butterscotch Icing (see below).

SERVES 6 TO 8

BUTTERSCOTCH ICING
◆

½ cup (1 stick) unsalted butter or margarine

1 cup brown sugar

¼ teaspoon salt

¼ cup milk

2 cups confectioners' sugar

1. Melt the butter in a small saucepan over low heat. Stir in the brown sugar and salt. Boil for 2 minutes, stirring constantly. Add the milk and bring to a full boil again. Cool to lukewarm.

2. Add the sugar and beat until smooth.

MAKES ENOUGH TO ICE TWO 8-INCH LAYERS OR ONE 9 × 13-INCH FLAT CAKE

Huge amounts of vegetarian food are prepared and served each day at this ashram in southern Virginia. The simplicity of the cooking complements the daily meditation and yoga offered at this large community of followers of Sri Swami Satchidananda. The highlight of a visit here, however, is the Lotus Shrine, built in the shape of a lotus flower—an ancient symbol for the spiritual unfolding of the soul. This spectacular shrine represents "all known faiths and faiths yet unknown," and its upper level has a column of light rising from the central altar. At the dome the light separates into twelve rays to illuminate an altar dedicated to each major faith. Quotations at each altar remind one that each faith has the same light as its source. Our favorite recipe from Yogaville is the carrot *payasam,* or pudding, which was served after an evening of devotional chanting with the community—a sweet ending to such inspiring song.

Yogaville

Satchidananda Ashram
Buckingham, Virginia

AN INDIAN DINNER

◆

Matar Panir

Kosumbri

Lemon Rice

Carrot Payasam

THE MEAL PRAYER, ANNA POORNE

OM Beloved Mother Nature,
You are here on our table as our food.
You are endlessly bountiful,
Benefactress of all.
Please grant us health and
   strength, wisdom, and dispassion
   to find permanent peace and joy,
   and to share this peace and joy
   with one and all.
Mother Nature is my mother.
My Father is the Lord of all.
All the peoples are my relatives.
The entire universe is my home.

I offer this unto OM
That Truth which is universal.

May the entire universe be filled
with Peace and Joy, Love and Light.

MATAR PANIR

◆

32 ounces yogurt
2 teaspoons cumin seeds
2 small onions, minced
2 tablespoons oil or ghee (clarified butter)
½ teaspoon cayenne
2 teaspoons ground turmeric
2 teaspoons salt
2 teaspoons ground coriander
2 teaspoons minced fresh ginger
1 teaspoon garam masala (see Note)
3 cups diced tomato
1½ pounds peas

1. Suspend the yogurt in cheesecloth over a bowl to catch the liquid. Then place the strained yogurt in the refrigerator for 4 hours (discard the liquid). Once it has hardened, cut the *panir* (as it is now called) into cubes and lightly toast them in the oven.

2. Toast the cumin seeds in a dry skillet.

3. Cook the minced onion in ghee.

4. Add to the onion everything but the peas and *panir*.

5. Simmer for 30 minutes. Add the peas and *panir*. Simmer for 10 minutes.

SERVES 8

NOTE *Garam masala* may be found in health-food stores or Indian grocery stores.

KOSUMBRI

◆

This south Indian condiment is traditionally served during Tamil New Year.

1 tablespoon black or brown mustard seed (see Note)

1 tablespoon channa dal *(see Note)*

1 tablespoon urad dal *(see Note)*

2 cups minced carrots

3 cups seeded, minced, salted, and drained cucumber

½ cup minced fresh cilantro

    Juice of 1 or 2 limes (depending on size)

    Salt to taste (lightly, please)

1. Sauté the spices briefly in a little oil.
2. Add the carrots, cucumber, cilantro, lime juice, and salt.

SERVES 4 TO 6

NOTE Black or brown mustard seeds and the *dals* may be found in health-food stores or Indian grocery stores.

LEMON RICE

◆

2 tablespoons sesame oil or ghee (clarified butter)

1 medium onion, minced

2 tablespoons black or brown mustard seeds

5 cups raw basmati rice, steamed

1½ teaspoons ground turmeric

4 cups boiling water

6 tablespoons lemon juice (fresh-squeezed is best)

1 cup peanuts or cashews, toasted

¼ cup coarsely minced fresh cilantro

1. Heat the oil and sauté the onion and mustard seeds until the mustard seeds turn gray and pop.

2. Stir in the rice, turmeric, and the boiling water. Bring back to a boil. Cover and reduce the heat. Simmer for 20 minutes.

3. Add the lemon juice, cashews, and cilantro and mix lightly. Cover and set aside for 5 minutes, then serve.

SERVES 10

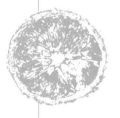

CARROT *PAYASAM* (PUDDING)

◆

¼ *cup blanched almonds*

¼ *cup* channa dal

1 *cup grated carrot*

2 *cups 2-percent milk*

¾ *cup sugar*

¼ *teaspoon ground cardamom*

⅛ *teaspoon saffron, dissolved*

6 *ounces evaporated milk*

1. Blend the almonds with water until the mixture has the consistency of pancake batter.

2. Lightly toast the *channa dal* in a dry skillet. Soak in water for an hour, drain, and blend with fresh water to achieve a thick batter.

3. Puree the carrot in a food processor. Simmer the carrot puree in milk until the mixture has thickened slightly and all the liquid has been absorbed.

4. Add the sugar to the carrot mixture, followed by the almond and *dal* batters.

5. Add the cardamom, saffron, and evaporated milk.

6. Chill for at least 4 hours. The mixture will be liquidy at first but will firm up when cold.

SERVES 8 TO 10

A WINTER MEAL

Spinach-Chard Soup

Stuffed Acorn Squash

Braised Red Cabbage

Pear Crisp

It's unusual to have a spiritual center renowned for its food, but the Zen Center of San Francisco, and its Tassajara and Green Gulch centers and its Greens restaurant in San Francisco are unique in this way. The gorgeous gardens at Green Gulch supply much of the food used at each place, and over the years the various chefs have published many cookbooks as they developed and refined recipes for their centers. We include here a meal that will not disappoint your expectations, just as time at each of these visually stunning Buddhist centers provides spiritual nourishment for those in search of it.

SPINACH-CHARD SOUP

◆

2 pounds mixed spinach and chard (you
  can also use just one or the other)

2 small yellow onions, sliced

1 tablespoon soy oil or light olive oil

½ teaspoon salt

2 garlic cloves, minced, plus 2 whole garlic cloves

3 tablespoons nutritional yeast (optional)

  Salt and white pepper

1 carrot, peeled and coarsely chopped

1 onion, peeled and coarsely chopped

2 stalks celery

1 potato, coarsely chopped

1 bay leaf

  A few peppercorns

1. Wash the spinach and chard carefully, making sure no grit remains. Chop coarsely.

2. Sauté the onion in the oil for a few minutes, until it turns translucent. Add the salt, minced garlic, and nutritional yeast and continue cooking for another 5 minutes. Add the greens, cover, and steam them until they are wilted, stirring occasionally.

3. To make the stock, bring to a boil ½ gallon of water, the carrot, onion, celery, potato, bay leaf, 2 whole cloves of garlic, and the peppercorns; simmer for 45 minutes; strain.

4. Add the stock to the greens and onion, and simmer until the greens are soft. Blend and season to taste with salt and white pepper.

SERVES 4 TO 6

VARIATION   After blending the soup, return to the stove and add I cup of grated cheese (Parmesan, Asiago, Romano, or Cheddar).

STUFFED ACORN SQUASH

◆

2 to 3 acorn squash

Garlic oil or butter

Salt to taste

1 large onion, chopped fine

½ pound mushrooms, chopped

1 to 2 stalks celery, chopped

1 to 2 garlic cloves, crushed

Dried thyme

Dried sage

½ cup white wine

¼ cup walnuts, roasted and chopped

¼ cup sunflower seeds

1 cup bread crumbs

1 cup cottage cheese

½ cup grated Cheddar cheese (optional)

Pepper to taste

1. Preheat the oven to 350°F.

2. Wash the squash and cut them in half. Scoop out the seeds, brush the squash with oil or butter, and lightly salt. Bake on a cookie sheet until a knife goes through easily but the squash is not quite done (30 to 40 minutes, depending on the size of the squash and the oven).

3. Sauté the onion, mushrooms, celery, and garlic in oil, adding salt to taste and the dried herbs.

4. When the onion is translucent, add the wine and cook until the vegetables are done.

5. Remove from the pan and add the nuts, seeds, bread crumbs, and cheeses. Taste for salt and pepper.

6. Fill the cooked squash generously with the stuffing, oil again, and return to the oven until the stuffing is heated through, approximately 15 minutes.

SERVES 4 TO 6

BRAISED RED CABBAGE

◆

1 medium red cabbage

1 medium red onion

2 to 3 garlic cloves, crushed or minced

   Olive oil

   Salt to taste

3 tablespoons lemon juice

   Balsamic vinegar

1 to 2 tablespoons poppy seeds

   Pepper to taste

1. Core the cabbage and slice thin. Set aside.

2. Slice the red onion into thin "half-moons."

3. In a skillet, sauté the onion with the garlic in a little olive oil (just enough to cover the bottom of the pan shallowly) with a pinch or two of salt. When the onion begins to become translucent, add the cabbage and the lemon juice. Cook over a medium flame until the cabbage is almost done. Add vinegar to taste and cook completely. Toss in the poppy seeds and salt and pepper to taste.

SERVES 4 TO 6

VARIATION   The above recipe is very plain—suitable as a side dish for more complicated meals. To make the dish more festive, add a sliced apple and a cup of walnuts (roasted and broken into large pieces) at the same time that you add the vinegar. Just before serving, add a cup of crumbled goat cheese or sour cream.

PEAR CRISP

◆

8 *ripe but still firm pears*

2 *tablespoons lemon juice*

1 *cup rolled oats*

$\frac{1}{2}$ *cup white unbleached flour*

$\frac{1}{2}$ *teaspoon salt*

2 *teaspoons ground cinnamon*

$\frac{1}{2}$ *cup brown sugar*

$\frac{1}{2}$ *cup toasted and chopped nuts (optional)*

$\frac{1}{2}$ *cup (1 stick) unsalted butter*

1. Preheat the oven to 375°F.

2. Wash the pears, core them, and cut them into chunks (peeling is unnecessary).

3. Toss them in the lemon juice, then place them in a 9 × 13-inch ovenproof baking dish.

4. Mix the rest of the ingredients together, cutting in the butter.

5. Spread over the pears, press down lightly, and put in the oven. Bake for 30 to 40 minutes, or until the fruit is soft. This is great served warm or hot with ice cream or whipped cream.

SERVES 4 TO 6

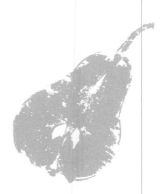

BENEDICTION

Fairburn Farm

Duncan,
British Columbia

A COUNTRY
BREAKFAST

◆

Fresh juice, Fruit, milk

Granola with Honey or
Brown Sugar

Delicious Bran Muffins

Buttermilk Pancakes

Food at this one-hundred-year-old family farm on Vancouver Island is intertwined with every moment of the family's lives. Darrel and Anthea Archer raise lambs, milk cows, tend chickens, and cultivate oats, barley, wheat, and garden vegetables. They churn butter for their own milk and use flour from the home-grown wheat for bread and scones. Jams and jellies are produced from their fruit trees, eggs from their chickens. Anthea's essay about food at the farm describes the spirit here so perfectly, I decided not to change a word of it. Though our travels were supposed to be confined to the United States, we strayed over the border to visit this country retreat when friends insisted we'd be delighted. We were! For this we send them many blessings!

Here is Anthea Archer's essay:

For twelve years I followed the tradition established by my mother-in-law, Mollie Archer, of offering three meals of nature's fresh bounty each day to our guests. Although this is rewarding in every aspect, it is also tiring when raising a family, and I eventually felt it was time to send forth our guests to sample the culinary presentations of several excellent local restaurants that offer the usual North American fare. I still prepare meals for advance bookings of ten or more, and this coincides perfectly with family reunions, retreats for friends, or any other occasions on which a group of like-minded people choose to stay at Fairburn for a few days. A rare treat is alfresco dining on the large veranda enjoying the cool of the evening.

Breakfast follows the tradition of coffee by 7:30 for those returning from an early walk in the fresh morning air by the mountain stream—an invigorating job—or for those just relaxing and enjoying the dawn on the large veranda. The aroma of baking muffins wafts through the house, making breakfast tempting, even for those who "never eat anything in the morning." There is fresh orange and grapefruit juice (unfortunately not from home-grown fruit) and apple juice from our orchard in season. The muffins vary daily—they may be bran, maple, oatmeal, blueberry, banana, or mixed fruit. As a family we eat old-fashioned porridge (oatmeal) each morning, summer and winter, and homemade granola, alone or sprinkled on the oatmeal. For those less adventurous, there is also a selection of popular cereals, some wholesome and others that become wholesome only if covered with fruit and milk. There is always a selection of fresh fruit or fruit salad. If desired, at this point, there is a daily choice, ranging from bacon and eggs (bacon from our Tamworth pigs and eggs from our free-range Plymouth Barred Rock hens), to vegetable frittata, French omelet, with accompanying whole-wheat bread (we grow our own wheat, which I grind for flour) and meadow-sweet butter from our Brown Swiss cow, buttermilk pancakes with maple syrup, or sourdough pancakes, sometimes with homemade sausage. If they take care not to eat too much, guests are then ready for a long hike or tour of the area, sometimes missing lunch. There are herb teas and a choice of black teas available throughout the day.

GRANOLA

◆

5 cups of any whole grain (e.g., cracked wheat,
rolled oats, rolled wheat)

1 cup flaked coconut (optional)

1 cup wheat germ

1 cup sunflower seeds, walnuts, pecans,
sesame seeds, or any combination

1 cup raisins, currants, chopped apricots,
or any combination

1 cup liquid honey

½ cup canola oil

1. Preheat the oven to 350°F.

2. Mix together the grain, coconut, wheat germ, seeds and nuts, and raisins. Melt the honey and oil together and pour over the cereal, mixing well.

3. Bake on large cookie sheets for 15 minutes. Add the raisins and return to the oven. Bake, stirring occasionally, until the granola is as brown as you prefer. (Sometimes I leave the granola in the oven longer than I plan, and sometimes other constraints force me to undercook the granola. I have had rave reviews in both cases—it is a very personal choice. Similarly, you can adjust quantities to taste, and some people do not put any oil in at all.)

DELICIOUS BRAN MUFFINS

◆

Handed down from a special friend.

Mix and set aside:

$1\frac{1}{2}$ *cups buttermilk*

$1\frac{1}{2}$ *cups natural bran*

Beat together:

$\frac{1}{2}$ *cup oil*

2 eggs

$\frac{1}{2}$ *cup granulated sugar*

$\frac{1}{2}$ *cup brown sugar*

Add the following to the ingredients in step 2 and beat well:

$\frac{1}{2}$ *teaspoon vanilla extract*

$1\frac{1}{2}$ *teaspoons baking soda*

$\frac{1}{2}$ *cup raisins*

Mix the egg mixture into the buttermilk and bran; then fold in the following:

$1\frac{1}{2}$ *cups unbleached white or whole-wheat flour*

$1\frac{1}{2}$ *teaspoons baking powder*

Bake at 350°F. for 25 minutes.

MAKES APPROXIMATELY 2 DOZEN MUFFINS

BUTTERMILK PANCAKES

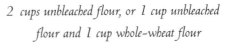

♦

Good on their own, with meadow-sweet butter, pure maple syrup, or fresh berries from the garden.

2 cups unbleached flour, or 1 cup unbleached
flour and 1 cup whole-wheat flour

1 teaspoon baking soda

½ teaspoon salt

1 tablespoon sugar or warmed honey

1 egg, well beaten

2 cups buttermilk or milk soured with lemon or vinegar

1½ tablespoons melted shortening or oil

Into the sifted dry ingredients, add the egg beaten into the milk, then the melted shortening. On a nonstick or lightly oiled pan (temperature at least 375° F.), ladle the batter in rounds of desired size. I like them small. Let them cook until bubbles appear on the surface, flip the pancakes, and cook for 2 or 3 minutes, or until cooked through. You can add fresh berries or a berry sauce, made by heating berries with a little honey.

SERVES 6

An evening meal should not be rushed. However, when the trees bend and sway, beckoning you into their peaceful embrace, even good, wholesome food deserves only so much lingering attention. Real life is where the food is grown—the fields with waving heads of wheat; the garden verdant with braccicas, greens, beans, rows of corn; the orchard of gnarled apple trees still producing well after eighty years; the clear-flowing spring where watercress raises its head. The most popular choice for the main course is lamb raised at Fairburn. Our reputation for "good lamb" is solid and rests on the lambs' quality of life even to the end. Mint sauce, made the old Lancashire way, helps too.

Dinners at Fairburn always begin with homemade soup and buns. Soups are made with meat or vegetable stocks or home-grown canned tomatoes. Even throughout the winter, as a family, we enjoy soups from vegetables frozen the previous autumn. The salad course always includes freshly picked spinach, leaf lettuce, iceberg lettuce, or romaine. Other greens are added, such as French sorrel, young leaves from raspberry or black currant bushes, scented geraniums, and, of course, an assortment of herbs chosen according to our mood. Mint is always a favorite of mine in a salad—not too much, just enough to impart a subtle flavor—and golden oregano is another favorite, together with chives (the young stems and flower buds), plus other edible flowers such as johnny-jump-ups, which smile up from the plate, calendula petals, and many herb flowers. The dressing varies, from a homemade Italian vinaigrette to a mayonnaise made with fresh eggs, oil, and herbs blended together, to Darrel's

SUNDAY DINNER

•

Garden Vegetable Soup

green salad with Darrel's Favorite Dressing

Fairburn Farm Lamb with Mint Sauce

Raspberry Pudding

favorite cooked mustard dressing. Though the main course features lamb, our meals allow equal time for many garden vegetables—in fact, vegetarians who stay feel the vegetables are enough by themselves without a special "vegetarian" dish.

GARDEN VEGETABLE SOUP

◆

Begin with a wholesome stock. The most economical way is to save washed ends of carrots and celery or any pieces of vegetable that are usually thrown away. Include only small quantities of strong-flavored vegetables such as turnip, which would predominate over the rest. Add a few peppercorns, a clove, a blade of mace, a bay leaf, or a mixture of fresh or dried herbs. Cover with water, place a lid on the pan, and simmer gently until a good flavor is obtained, approximately half an hour, depending upon the type and size of vegetable pieces. If you leave the pan too long, the water will evaporate. If you don't object to meat, you can include a marrow bone or chicken carcass for added flavor. Drain through a sieve and use the stock as a basis for soups or for adding to sauces or any dishes that require stock.

When I make soup other than our own canned tomato soup or a specific soup such as asparagus or green pea soup, I gather the vegetables left from the previous evening, and I always make lots so I can do this. Sometimes I chop the vegetables, other times I blend them with a little stock and if necessary add a tablespoon of flour when I blend, as well as fresh herbs. My soups are never the same two days in a row. If you have mainly broccoli or broccoli that is about to bolt, put this in the soup and add some Cheddar or other favorite cheese. Italian mozzarella can be too stringy, but this makes for interesting eating and it is often used in French onion soup. When in doubt, test with a teaspoon for salt and pepper seasoning if you feel the herbs have not filled the bill.

Enjoy your soup; it is your own creation. Be proud of it.

DARREL'S FAVORITE DRESSING

I have been given this recipe with variations by several guests, but this one gets the highest rating.

> ½ cup vinegar
>
> 1 cup water
>
> 2 tablespoons unbleached white flour
>
> 1 cup white sugar
>
> ¾ teaspoon salt
>
> 1 tablespoon dry mustard
>
> 2 eggs
>
> 1 cup whole milk

Heat the vinegar and water. In a separate bowl, blend the flour, sugar, salt, and mustard. Beat the eggs somewhat and blend with the milk, then stir them into the dry ingredients carefully (my advice is to keep stirring and it will mix well), then add the mixture to the hot water and vinegar. I cook this dressing in a double boiler; then, if the phone rings or a guest needs me, I can turn off the heat and nothing is spoiled. Keep stirring until it thickens. Let it cool and it will keep in your fridge for a long time.

FAIRBURN FARM LAMB

◆

This recipe is almost too simple to include. Our lamb is delicious enough to stand alone, with no added mustard-and-flour paste, no garlic slivers inserted throughout the meat—these are necessary only to cover up a poor flavor.

I take a 6-pound lamb leg from the freezer around 3:00 P.M. and place it in a roasting pan with over ½ inch of water and sometimes a sprig of rosemary. I dust the roast with our own whole-wheat flour—just enough to cover—and place it in the oven, uncovered, at 350° F. I check from time to time to make sure that some water remains, for this is the basis of a good gravy. Around 6:30 the lamb is ready. I let it sit for 10 minutes, being sure to keep it hot. (Lamb should always be served hot.) My advice is have someone serve the vegetables and, as the lamb is carved, place it on the individual plates, add gravy (prepared while the roast was sitting), and serve immediately with mint sauce on the table.

SERVES AT LEAST 8

MINT SAUCE

◆

Pick a handful of fresh mint—the top sprigs of leaves are best. Pull the stems and place the leaves in a blender. Add 2 tablespoons of boiling water and 1 teaspoon of sugar. Blend until mixed. Cover with malt vinegar and mix again. Store in a covered jar in the fridge. Serve in a glass bowl with a small spoon.

RASPBERRY PUDDING

◆

The name "raspberry pudding" sounds rather heavy, but this is a good rich dessert—not at all stodgy. You can use any fruit, fresh or frozen, and the topping is almost meringuelike, unless, like my mother-in-law, you decide there is too much sugar, in which case it will be a cake topping but still very yummy.

2 to 3 cups fresh raspberries (or defrosted frozen)

1 cup plus 2 tablespoons unbleached flour white

2 cups plus 2 tablespoons sugar

2 tablespoons unsalted butter, quite cold

5 tablespoons sweet butter, at room temperature

1 egg

1 teaspoon baking powder

½ teaspoon salt

⅓ cup milk

Preheat the oven to 350°F.

Spread the fruit on the bottom of a buttered and floured cake pan, preferably a 9 × 9-inch Pyrex pan. Sprinkle 2 tablespoons of flour and 2 tablespoons of sugar over the fruit (if defrosting fruit, blend the sugar and flour into the juice before pouring it over the fruit in the pan). Cut the 2 tablespoons of cold butter over the fruit in paper-thin slices.

Cream the 5 tablespoons of butter and remaining 2 cups of sugar; blend in the egg. Sift the cup of flour, baking powder, and salt, and add to the creamed mixture alternately with the milk. Beat well. Drop the batter in spoonfuls over the fruit. Bake for about ½ hour. Serve warm or cold, with fresh cream or ice cream, topping with a few whole berries.

SERVES 6 TO 8

Names and Addresses

♦

Abbey of Gethsemani
Trappist, KY 40051

Abbey of New Clairvaux
Seventh and C Streets
Vina, CA 96092

All Saints Episcopal Convent
PO Box 3127
Catonsville, MD 21228

Avila Retreat Center
711 Mason Road
Durham, NC 27712

Bhavana Society
Route 1, Box 218-3
High View, WV 26808

Breitenbush Hot Springs
PO Box 578
Detroit, OR 97342

Camp Weed and Cerveny
Conference Center
Route 3, Box 140
Live Oak, FL 32060

Dai Bosatsu Zendo
HCR 1, Box 171
Livingston Manor, NY 12758

Fairburn Farm
3310 Jackson Road, RR7
Duncan, BC V9L4N4, Canada

Falkynor Farm
PO Box 290057
Davie, FL 33329

Healing Center of Arizona
25 Wilson Canyon Road
Sedona, AZ 86336

The Hermitage Community
11321 Dutch Settlement
Three Rivers, MI 49093

Holy Name Monastery
PO Box H
33201 State Road 52
St. Leo, FL 33574

Immaculate Heart Community
888 San Ysidro Lane
Santa Barbara, CA 93108

Insight Meditation Society
1230 Pleasant Street
Barre, MA 01005

Isis Oasis
20889 Geyserville Avenue
Geyserville, CA 95441

Mepkin Abbey
1098 Mepkin Abbey Road
Moncks Corner, SC 29461

New Orleans Zen Temple
748 Camp Street
New Orleans, LA 70130

Pendle Hill
338 Plush Mill Road
Wallingford, PA 19086

Portsmouth Abbey
Portsmouth, RI 02871

Rancho La Puerta
PO Box 463057
Escondido, CA 92046

Rose Hill
PO Box 3126
Aiken, SC 29802

St. Christopher
Conference Center
2810 Seabrook Island Road
Johns Island, SC 29455

St. Francis Friends of the Poor
135 W. 31st Street
New York, NY 10001

St. Mary's Episcopal Retreat
& Conference Center
PO Box 188
Sewanee, TN 37375

Southern Dharma
Retreat Center
Route 1, Box 34H
Hot Springs, NC 28743

Springwater Center
7179 Mill Street
Springwater, NY 14560

Transfiguration Monastery
701 N.Y. Route 79
Windsor, NY 13865

Villa Maria Del Mar
2-1918 E. Cliff Drive
Santa Cruz, CA 95062

Visitation Monastery
2300 Spring Hill Avenue
Mobile, AL 36607

Wakulla Springs Lodge
One Springs Drive
Wakulla Springs, FL 32305

Wellspring Renewal Center
PO Box 332
Philo, CA 95466

Yogaville
Satchidananda Ashram
Buckingham, Virginia 23921

Zen Center of San Francisco
300 Page Street
San Francisco, CA 94102

SPECIAL TREATS

◆

Many monasteries help support themselves with food made in their kitchens. The Abbey of the Genesee, for example, makes thirty thousand loaves a week of its famous Monk's Bread. Here are a few memorable treats from monasteries that we couldn't get the recipes for but that are available via mail order:

Butterscotch Fruitcake
Abbey of the Genesee,
3258 River Road, Piffard, NY 14533
(716) 243-2220

Trappist Cheese
Abbey of Gethsemani,
Trappist, KY 40051
(502) 549-3117

Butternut Munch Candy
Mount St. Mary's Abbey,
300 Arnold Road, Wrentham, MA 02093
(508) 528-1282

Wrapped Caramels
Our Lady of the Mississippi Abbey,
Dubuque, IA 52003
(319) 582-2595

Saint Benedict Wines
Transfiguration Monastery,
701 N.Y. Route 79, Windsor, NY 13865
(607) 655-2366

ABOUT THE AUTHOR

•

MARCIA M. KELLY is the author, with her husband Jack, of the popular series *Sanctuaries: A Guide to Lodgings in Monasteries, Abbeys, and Retreats of the United States,* and the editor of *One Hundred Graces: Mealtime Blessings.* Their research for these books and also this volume of recipes has take them to more than two hundred and fifty monasteries, abbeys, and retreats. The Kellys live in New York.

OTHER BELL TOWER BOOKS

Books that nourish the soul, illuminate the mind,
and speak directly to the heart.

◆

Valeria Alfeyeva
PILGRIMAGE TO DZHVARI
A Woman's Journey of Spiritual Awakening
An unforgettable introduction to the riches of the Eastern Orthodox
mystical tradition. A modern *Way of a Pilgrim.*
0-517-88389-9 Softcover

Tracy Cochran and Jeff Zaleski
TRANSFORMATIONS
Awakening to the Sacred in Ourselves
An exploration of enlightenment experiences and the ways
in which they can transform our lives.
0-517-70150-2 Hardcover

David A. Cooper
ENTERING THE SACRED MOUNTAIN
Exploring the Mystical Practices of Judaism, Buddhism, and Sufism
An inspiring chronicle of one man's search for truth.
0-517-88464-X Softcover

David A. Cooper
THE HEART OF STILLNESS
The Elements of Spiritual Practice
A comprehensive guidebook to the principles of inner work.
0-517-88187-X Softcover

David A. Cooper
SILENCE, SIMPLICITY, AND SOLITUDE
A Guide for Spiritual Retreat
Required reading for anyone contemplating a retreat.
0-517-88186-1 Softcover

Marc David
NOURISHING WISDOM
A Mind/Body Approach to Nutrition and Well-Being
A book that advocates awareness in eating.
0-517-88129-2 Softcover

Kat Duff
THE ALCHEMY OF ILLNESS
A luminous inquiry into the function and purpose of illness.
0-517-88097-0 Softcover

Noela N. Evans
MEDITATIONS FOR THE PASSAGES AND
CELEBRATIONS OF LIFE
A Book of Vigils
Articulating the often unspoken emotions experienced
at such times as birth, death, and marriage.
0-517-59341-6 Hardcover
0-517-88299-X Softcover

Bernard Glassman & Rick Fields
INSTRUCTIONS TO THE COOK
A Zen Master's Lessons in Living a Life that Matters
A distillation of Zen wisdom that can be used equally well as
a manual on business or spiritual practice, cooking or life.
0-517-70377-7 Hardcover

Burghild Nina Holzer
A WALK BETWEEN HEAVEN AND EARTH
A Personal Journal on Writing and the Creative Process
How keeping a journal focuses and expands our awareness
of ourselves and everything that touches our lives.
0-517-88096-2 Softcover

Greg Johanson and Ron Kurtz
GRACE UNFOLDING
Psychotherapy in the Spirit of the Tao-te ching
The interaction of client and therapist illuminated
through the gentle power and wisdom of Lao Tsu's ancient classic.
0-517-88130-6 Softcover

Selected by Marcia and Jack Kelly
ONE HUNDRED GRACES
Mealtime Blessings
A collection of graces from many traditions, inscribed in calligraphy
reminiscent of the manuscripts of medieval Europe.
0-517-58567-7 Hardcover
0-517-88230-2 Softcover

Jack and Marcia Kelly
SANCTUARIES
A Guide to Lodgings in Monasteries, Abbeys, and
Retreats of the United States
For those in search of renewal and a little peace;
described by the *New York Times* as "the *Michelin Guide* of the retreat set."
THE NORTHEAST *0-517-57727-5 Softcover*
THE WEST COAST & SOUTHWEST *0-517-88007-5 Softcover*
THE COMPLETE U.S. *0-517-88517-4 Softcover*

Barbara Lachman
THE JOURNAL OF HILDEGARD OF BINGEN
A year in the life of the twelfth-century German saint—
the diary she never had the time to write herself.
0-517-59169-3 Hardcover
0-517-88390-2 Softcover

Katharine Le Mée
CHANT
The Origins, Form, Practice, and Healing Power of Gregorian Chant
The ways in which this ancient liturgy
can nourish us and transform our lives.
0-517-70037-9 Hardcover

Gunilla Norris
BECOMING BREAD
Meditations on Loving and Transformation
A book linking the food of the spirit—love—
with the food of the body—bread.
0-517-59168-5 Hardcover

Gunilla Norris
BEING HOME
A Book of Meditations
An exquisite modern book of hours,
a celebration of mindfulness in everyday activities.
0-517-58159-0 Hardcover

Gunilla Norris
JOURNEYING IN PLACE
Reflections from a Country Garden
Another classic book of meditations
illuminating the sacredness of daily experience.
0-517-59762-4 Hardcover

Gunilla Norris
SHARING SILENCE
Meditation Practice and Mindful Living
A book describing the essential conditions
for meditating in a group or on one's own.
0-517-59506-0 Hardcover

Ram Dass and Mirabai Bush
COMPASSION IN ACTION
Setting Out on the Path of Service
Heartfelt encouragement and advice for those ready
to commit time and energy to relieving suffering in the world.
0-517-88500-X Softcover

His Holiness Shantanand Saraswati
THE MAN WHO WANTED TO MEET GOD
Myths and Stories that Explain the Inexplicable
The teaching stories of one of India's greatest living saints.
0-517-88520-4 Softcover

Rabbi Rami M. Shapiro
WISDOM OF THE JEWISH SAGES
A Modern Reading of Pirke Avot
A third-century treasury of maxims on justice, integrity, and virtue—
Judaism's principal ethical scripture.
0-517-79966-9 Hardcover

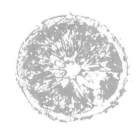

Joan Tollifson
BARE-BONES MEDITATION
Waking Up from the Story of My Life
An unvarnished, exhilarating account of one woman's struggle
to make sense of her life.
0-517-88792-4 Softcover

Ed. Richard Whelan
SELF-RELIANCE
The Wisdom of Ralph Waldo Emerson
as Inspiration for Daily Living
A distillation of Emerson's spiritual writings for contemporary readers.
0-517-58512-X Softcover

Bell Tower books are for sale at your local bookstore
or you may call Random House at 1-800-793-BOOK to order with a credit card.